W9-DHU-117

Clashing Symbols

An Introduction to Faith and Culture

MICHAEL PAUL GALLAGHER, S.J.

PAULIST PRESS
New York / Mahwah, N.J.

The Publisher gratefully acknowledges use of the following. Excerpt from "In Illo Tempore" from *Station Island* by Seamus Heaney. Copyright 1984 by Seamus Heaney. Reprinted by permission of Farrar, Straus & Giroux, Inc. and Faber and Faber, Ltd.

Cover design by James F. Brisson

Cover art: Montage by James F. Brisson based on 12th century Byzantine mosaic and Georges Rouault's "Sainte Face"

Library of Congress Cataloging-in-Publication Data

Gallagher, Michael Paul.
    Clashing symbols : an introduction to faith & culture / by Michael Paul Gallagher.
        p.   cm.
    Includes bibliographical references.
    ISBN 0-8091-3784-4 (alk. paper)
    1. Christianity and culture. 2. Catholic Church—History—20th century. I. Title.
BR115.C8G27   1998
261—dc21   97-33968
                                                                 CIP

Published by Paulist Press
997 Macarthur Boulevard
Mahwah, New Jersey 07430

Printed and bound in the
United States of America

Contents

Preface to the American Edition

Since I now divide my working year between Rome and Dublin, I see many American tourists in both cities. Recently I began to notice a difference between how they behave in the two settings. In Rome they tend to stand at street corners with maps, sometimes looking worried, sometimes in animated discussion with one another. In Dublin they may carry maps but are more likely to ask directions from people passing by. Indeed they seem to enjoy the opportunity to have contact with the locals. Is the difference simply one of language? That in Ireland English is the main language? Perhaps it is deeper than that. I think the American tourist is more at ease in Ireland because the whole culture, though very different from home, seems closer to them. Culture, in this sense, is like a hidden language rather than a spoken one.

This book is about the hidden grammar of the languages we live and about how to reflect on culture from a Christian perspective. It tries to alert people to the power of culture—influencing us for good or ill—and then to suggest ways of finding a certain serenity of faith within the complexity of today. Do we make culture or does culture make us? How can we wake up to its workings? How can we read our realities in the light of Christ?

The whole topic of culture has become a major debating point in North America in recent years. Sometimes it is seen in terms of multiculturalism. Last summer I walked up Fordham Road in the Bronx one Saturday afternoon and was made dramatically aware of New York's cultural diversity in ways that would be impossible both in Ireland and in Italy. There must have been twenty different groups promoting some version of religion.

Another much discussed issue is the role of the "dominant culture" and the fact that the American entertainment industry has a virtual monopoly on the images that influence young people in the whole global village. This export of images, it has been argued, is perhaps more potent in shaping the future than the export of arms. The MTV networks now have a much larger audience outside the United States than at home.

A third American field of interest concerns the so-called "culture wars" and the realization that people within one nation can remain deeply divided over basic assumptions about existence. There has been an avalanche of writing on liberalism and whether it is a genuine and specifically American inheritance or a dangerous deception sapping at the roots of Christian faith. When does the dignity of the individual tumble into narrow individualism? Voices are raised in alarm that personal rights are being asserted in ways that degrade the real sense of the person: a cult of individual indulgence, we are told, has reached the point of being cultural suicide.

These pages approach such issues in a spirit of reflection rather than in a style of controversy. "At the heart of every culture lies the attitude a person takes to the greatest mystery, the mystery of God." Thus wrote Pope John Paul II in *Centesimus Annus* (#24). The aim of this book is to provide a double theology—of nonpanic and of liberation—for believers faced with their surrounding cultures. Nonpanic means reading the situation with spiritual wisdom but without complacency. We are all aware of the health hazard of blood pressure and heart fatigue—and of how a polluted environment can cause serious illness. There is a more subtle field of spiritual health, where dangers of culture put pressure on our hearts and can kidnap our hopes.

This book proposes a Christian ecology of the imagination and hopes to offer a theology of cultural liberation. Insofar as we are free *from* the potentially negative forces in our culture, we will be truly free *for* faith, and for a creative Christian life that does not just discern culture but hopes to transform it in the light of the gospel.

When *Clashing Symbols* was published in London last year, friends commented to me that some of the early chapters make fairly demanding reading and that I should encourage readers to feel free to postpone the sections on theory and on church history, if they wish. I am told by these same reliable friends that the second half of the book flows more easily and even "gets exciting"! I hope so.

Introduction

Culture as Cinderella

> *We become more and more aware of the extent to which the baffling problem of 'culture' underlies the problems of the relation of every part of the world to every other.* (T. S. Eliot)[1]

> *A cultural matrix is a function ... of the conflicts between the inclinations toward conversion and the counter-pulls toward unconverted thinking, feeling, and living.* (Robert Doran)[2]

It has been said, provocatively, that the twentieth century began in 1917 and ended unexpectedly in 1989. Even if that remark does not apply equally to our whole planet, its point is clear: for some seventy years huge amounts of intellectual, economic and political energy were channelled into a confrontation between two ideological blocs – the capitalist and the communist. If that particular conflict now seems gone for good, other battlegrounds of clashing symbols have emerged.

As long as those older ideological confrontations divided the world, 'culture' was like a Cinderella waiting in the kitchen: her value was recognized by some but her public impact was small. To expand that fairy-tale into a mini-parable: 'Cultura' was kept in a subordinate position by the Ugly Sisters of Marxism and Atheism. These polemical sisters produced so much noise that the more subtle voice of Cultura remained unheard – until the arrival of the Fairy Godmother, Freedom, and the invitation by Prince History to the Ball celebrating the end of Modernity. Without forcing the details too much, this version of the Cinderella story suggests that a whole approach to reality was neglected in the era of dualist oppositions, and that as we leave behind the false clarities of 'modernity', the moment has come to appreciate culture as a more adequate way of interpreting the influences around us.

This Cinderella story is being rewritten within both secular and religious zones of reflection today. Within the Catholic Church, as will be seen, the concept has assumed enormous prominence in the years since the Second Vatican Council, and more particularly as a result of what Pope John Paul II has often described as a crucial area where our destiny is at stake. Within other Churches too the cultural dimension has come to the fore as a topic of crucial importance today: thus the World Council of Churches is engaged in a long-term study of the relation between the gospel and cultures (as will be seen later).

Cultural change and cultural conflict

No doubt the fall of the Berlin Wall was the event that best symbolized the end of one cultural epoch and the inauguration of something new. Many people may remember a strange scene that was shown on television screens during that celebrated year of 1989: the rather gentle lowering to the ground of statues of Lenin or Marx in various countries of the communist bloc. And the empty pedestals raised various questions. What will take their place? Will more invisible idols come to power?

1989 has come to symbolize the death certificate of modernity and the confirmation of the transition to so-called postmodernity – a cultural phase that claims various birthdays, ranging from as early as Nietzsche's philosophy to the social and political upheavals of the year 1968. During modernity we had expressed our commitments according to one or other ideological stance. With postmodernity we entered into a phase of unknowing, no longer sure of how to define ourselves, or whether it is even possible. This agnosticism was magnificently evoked in a recent masterpiece of cinema by the Greek director Theo Angelopoulos. *The Gaze of Ulysses* is about searching for lost images, where one long sequence shows a huge statue of Lenin travelling with slow dignity down a river, as people standing on the banks cross themselves as if witnessing a religious procession. But the film, set in part amid the violence of Sarajevo, captures both the lonely quest that marks this postmodern moment of culture and some old cultural enmities coming to violent life again. Indeed the expression 'culture wars' has entered our vocabulary in recent years. It evokes opposed assumptions about values that frequently polarize people; one thinks of the debates between 'liberals' and 'conservatives' within the United States. More broadly it can point to the potential for prejudice and for propaganda wars that arise between the world's major culture blocs – most obviously between Islam and the so-called Christian West.

With the demise of artificially dividing walls, not only has culture emerged from the shadows in a positive sense: its darker potentials are also making themselves felt. We are all cultural animals, both in its humanizing and dehumanizing meanings. In an influential article, entitled 'The Clash of Civilizations?', Professor Samuel Huntington of Harvard University argued that future conflicts 'will not be primarily ideological or primarily economic. The great divisions among humankind and the dominating source of conflict will be cultural', and he added that cultural characteristics change less easily than political and economic ones. It is another way of expressing the Cinderella insight: 'the Velvet Curtain of culture has replaced the Iron Curtain of ideology as the most significant dividing line'.[3]

Cultural horizons of religion

There is a tendency to talk about a new world culture, with both positive and negative interpretations. The positive side is that in the 'global village', where one can see events within minutes on the television screen, a consensus can emerge that is more aware of injustices. The negative side is that precisely this image world of television can be a source of manipulation, trivialization, and ultimately an anti-culture of commercial superficiality. Worries abound that we are moving towards 'a single global culture' in line with the computerized information networks; but 'a memory-less culture' without identity and without history would be a contradiction.[4]

In spite of all this potential levelling, cultural groupings remain remarkably resistant to the homogenization of the global village. One need only think of some tendencies within Islam or Hinduism, where religious cultures have become assertive over self-identity, or of the ethnically rooted conflicts of the former Yugoslavia. In cultures as diverse as those of Africa or Japan, the repercussions of the global village seem marginal in comparison with the differentness that remains. Thus the impact of the media-culture of 'mascara and soap opera' (a phrase from Julia Kristeva) can be shallow in two senses: on the surface and silly. Where people are without strong anchors of belonging, television trash has a more dehumanizing impact. Any theory about the trivializing impact of the media has to take account of a contrary reality – the survival of deep cultural differences between peoples.

It is not only in the field of global analysis that 'culture' has emerged as a key concept in recent years. A relatively new discipline called cultural studies has arrived in many universities and merits a section to itself in more ambitious bookshops. One tendency here is to study culture as 'a moral activity' and to focus on the 'making of meaning' in contemporary society; it also tries to examine the interaction between power, values, mass media and imagination.[5] There is a widespread insistence that 'cultural studies' represents a radical break with the old stratifications between 'high' and 'low' culture and that it aims at more than a description of ways of life: it wants to investigate how the production and consumption of cultural images is controlled in different societies.

Culture, as a hidden censor of what is socially acceptable, has been another theme in recent reflection, as exemplified by the success of Stephen Carter's book *The Culture of Disbelief.* Since North American culture is rapidly becoming a presence in lived culture around the globe, Carter's argument is relevant beyond the borders of the United States or his particular specialization in constitutional law. In brief, he diagnoses how the pressures of contemporary culture keep religion impotent in the public sphere. The message is that 'it is perfectly all right to *believe* that stuff' provided you keep it to yourself; in other words, the only form of religion permitted becomes a 'trivialization of faith', something on the level of a hobby, but 'not really a fit activity for intelligent, public-spirited adults'.[6]

This kind of 'secular marginalization' (as it will be called in the chapter on cultural discernment) has also been a focus for theological reflection, because the very possibility of religious faith today is influenced by cultural factors. Our receptivity for revelation is more shaped by culture than by philosophical clarities. We seldom live by ideas or ideologies but rather by images of life communicated by our surrounding worlds. Hence the cultural wavelength is central for understanding the shifting currents within religious commitment now. As will be argued later, various forms of 'cultural unbelief' now constitute the main family of distance from faith or rejection of religion.

In a world of such pluralism, it becomes one of the tasks for theology to understand why the Christian vision, which had such eloquent and encompassing impact on people in the past, seems to have lost meaningfulness in today's cultural situation. The insight that cultural change influences the agenda of theology, was symbolized in the opening sentence of Bernard Lonergan's *Method in Theology*, with its claim that 'theology mediates between a cultural matrix and the significance and role of religion in that matrix'. And he then goes on to note that once the meaning of culture widens from the 'classicist notion' to the 'empirical notion of culture' as involving ways of life, then theology is no longer a matter of ageless or 'permanent achievement' but is recognized as 'an ongoing process'.[7] In his judgement the contemporary world is undergoing 'a crisis not of faith but of culture'.[8]

In addition there is a new centrality of culture within Church discourse, as different key words have come to prominence in Catholicism in these recent decades. Thus, 'dialogue' and then 'justice' were the new words of the sixties and seventies, followed by 'new evangelization' and 'culture' during the eighties and nineties. At the same time the relations between faith and culture have become the object of intense debate, especially with regard to 'inculturation'. Religion and culture have had a reciprocal relationship in every epoch of history until the recent centuries in the West. That the Western Christian Churches represent a small minority of Christian believers in the world has been known for decades. Now this inevitable demographic shift from the richer world is being seen as a cultural phenomenon that will gradually change our sense of religious identity. Within all the Christian Churches it is in non-Western countries that the most lively languages of faith are being born.

Complex and omnipresent

The phenomenon called culture is an exclusively human experience, as a simple example can show. Unlike many animals, a new-born infant has little genetic programming to guide its behaviour; instead of being able to survive on its own, the human baby needs others for a considerable time before arriving at independence. Culture is the human learning space where the child develops its open-ended potentials for growth. And, unlike the animals, this adventure of cultural learning is 'not simply about behaviour. It is also about ideas', involving patterns of meaning, embodied in symbols, and subject to considerable evolution and even conscious change.[9] From birth we are all surrounded by this omnipresent and seemingly omnipotent complex called culture, which is both external and internal, both observable and concealed.

The more one thinks about it, the field of culture seems full of contradictory tendencies. It does not point clearly and constantly in one direction. Instead it sends out contrary signals. Thus we speak in the one breath of the relativizing of Western culture and about the global village created by Western-style communications and technology. We talk about the rise of secular culture, but we are witnessing a surprising turn-around in this area. Thirty years ago many sociologists argued confidently about an 'irreversible secular-ization', predicting that religion would inevitably decline in influence and become something socially marginal. More recently we have heard about the 'return of religion', the rise of fundamen-talism, the claims of faith within the public sphere, the multiplying of new religious movements, and the many-faceted spiritual explor-ation called 'New Age'. Strangely, both the floating religiousness and the fundamentalist rigidity may have the same origin – a desire to escape complexity and find anchors. These seemingly contrary phenomena are provoked by the fragmentations, the malnutritions, and the rootless loneliness of a dominantly secular culture.

An unrecognized ocean

What is culture for our purposes in this book? The term is used here mainly in its broad anthropological meaning – as a cluster of assumptions, values and ways of life – rather than in its older and more elite meaning connected with intellectual or artistic activity. The next chapter will explore some of the many meanings associated with culture. Monsieur Jourdain, in Molière's *Le Bourgeois Gentilhomme*, made the much-mocked discovery that he had been speaking prose all his life and had not known it. What is comic is that his teacher had given him only a word and not an insight. We are all living within a culture but to grasp its significance involves a series of surprises and awakenings. One can clarify, as is often done, the enlargement of the term 'culture' from the sphere of thought or artistic expression or conscious human development, to the more inclusive sense of culture as indicating life-styles and assumptions. Though important as a starting point, this descriptive approach misses the power of culture as involving not simply a neutral cluster of behaviour patterns or values, but a hidden set of control mechanisms that shape our sensibility and our 'structure of feeling'.[10] Culture can be an unrecognized presence, 'a highly selective screen' between us and our world which decides 'what we pay attention to and what we ignore'.[11] Thus culture is quite simply the main influence on how we see ourselves (what contemporary theorists call our 'social imaginary'), and it is all the more potent for being largely concealed in its impact. In this sense the Marxist-style claim that context conditions consciousness remains valid: indeed the two-way traffic between the structure of our lives and the cultures we inhabit is a crucial insight in this whole area. The way we live or work shapes how we think and feel and in turn how we think and feel becomes a powerful reinforcer of how we picture our possibilities of changing this world or not.

Perhaps a series of metaphoric parallels can begin to evoke the inescapable role culture plays in shaping our sense of identity, because it forms our mind-sets and heart-sets and gives us our typical way of interpreting our lives.

Culture, therefore, is like:

- an ocean, surrounding us as water a fish;
- an environment that seems natural, especially if it is the only one we know;
- the air we breathe, that may be healthy or polluted;

- a lens, something we see through without realizing that it is not the only way of seeing;
- a transmitter sending almost subliminal messages, that affect our priorities without us knowing;
- a filter, allowing through certain images of normality but not others;
- a set of codes, like writing, which is artificial but comes to be second nature;
- a complex traffic light that signals what one should pay attention to;
- a language not just of words, but of expectations we learn to obey;
- a set of blinkers, censoring what can be seen;
- a cage that is there and not there, as in the acting of a mime artist who pretends to be inside a glass box;
- an iceberg of the common sense of a group, which stays largely submerged or unconscious;
- a baby's building bricks, the basis for creating a world;
- a flight recorder preserving the memory of humanity's journey;
- a life agenda that controls the conversation about existence;
- a womb, within which one feels perfectly at home, not knowing there are other worlds;
- an accumulation of unacknowledged habits, like an addiction that resists recognition;
- a conspiracy of silence, imposed by the past;
- a menu of existence, either 'fixed' or 'à la carte': either way the choices have limits;
- a playground of possibilities, inviting one to creative freedom;
- an ever-present horizon, beyond which one cannot see.

In this random litany of images there are tensions between evocations of being trapped and those that suggest space for movement. Both can be true of 'lived' culture: it can encourage creativity or it can prove imprisoning. What all these metaphors have in common is the crucial fact that culture is usually a hidden persuader in our lives. It involves a convergence of massaging messages (as Marshall McLuhan might say) that lull us into assuming that all this is natural, whereas the root meaning of culture – from *colere* in Latin, to till or cultivate – suggests that it is the opposite of natural. In fact it is whatever we have made – whether a Tower of Babel or a Sistine Chapel. It is a human invention over a long time. Although nothing about culture is necessary or inevitable, when we swim in this ocean or see through this lens or receive the transmission of this force around us, everything seems utterly normal and neutral. Awakening to its non-neutrality is a first step towards a Christian response to culture in practice.

Against the background of lively cultural debates in many fields, this book has a fairly modest scope: to present aspects of the faith-culture relationship as it has evolved within recent decades. The aim is to introduce the reader to the principal insights and controversies being discussed by both individual thinkers and Church bodies concerned with this theme. Early chapters explore the range of meaning of 'culture'. Next, some sections focus on Church developments in understanding and responding to culture. Themes concerning modernity and postmodernity are then given fairly extended treatment, especially from a religious point of view. The final four chapters deal with more 'pastoral' issues – inculturation, discernment, youth ministry and the outlines of a spirituality for today's culture.

The style of presentation is non-specialist and yet (as the notes show) the argument draws on the work of some leading thinkers in the field. In this way these pages should provide scaffolding, so to speak, for further reflection by students or groups who wish to understand the increasing relevance of culture for theology and for religious commitment today. The hope is also to help ordinary Christians to 'read' the realities and challenges of contemporary culture with wisdom, with confidence and in the light of faith.

Chapter One

Clarifying the Concept

> *Every culture does in fact educate its members, by commission or omission, to particular styles of feeling, toward the development of a rich range of affections and emotions or toward a limited or limiting vocabulary of feeling.* (Margaret Miles)[1]

> *Culture almost defies definition because it is a pervasive atmosphere rather than an articulated system.* (Avery Dulles)[2]

In the nineteenth century two famous accounts of culture appeared within two years of each other, and between them they point to two main schools of interpretation of this concept. In 1869 Matthew Arnold published *Culture and Anarchy* where he argued that culture meant 'the pursuit of perfection' which entailed 'an inward condition of the mind and spirit', a quality 'at variance with the mechanical and material civilisation' of that industrial age. In his view culture meant the 'pursuit of sweetness and light' through becoming acquainted with the best that has been thought and said in world history.[3]

By contrast, in 1871, the British anthropologist Edward Tylor published his pioneering work entitled *Primitive Culture*, where he offered one of the earliest of non-Arnoldian definitions of culture:

Culture or civilization is that complex whole which includes knowledge, belief, art, morals, law, custom, and any other capabilities and habits acquired by man as a member of society.[4]

Culture remains one of those words that can be exasperating in its inclusiveness. It can seem to be a chameleon-term that changes its significance depending on the user. But in fact most of its meanings offer variations on either the Arnold or the Tylor tradition. When Arnold wrote in that eloquent style, he could be fairly confident that 'cultured' people would understand him, even if those he called 'barbarians' might not. His elite audience shared with him a sense that culture pointed to the highest available expressions of human vision and human value. But to say that is to beg the question: who decides what is best? Obviously, the 'cultured'! Thus behind the Arnoldian theory lay a strangely circular field of argument: 'cultural' leaders had a monopoly on what 'culture' means. They exalted the 'classics' as models to be imitated. The very notion of having classic works of art implied permanent values, a core of stable excellence amid the changes of history. In short, this view of culture was traditional and normative, and it had prevailed in Western education for centuries.

In spite of Arnold, until fairly recently the word 'culture' was less widely used in English than in Latin languages. The French novelist André Malraux, who was Minister for Culture under General de Gaulle, said that culture is what answers our human questions about what we are doing here in this world. Every day a national radio news broadcast in Italy ends with 'la pagina culturale' – the cultural page, meaning some event in the world of art or music or books. However, the *Sunday Times* publishes a fat weekly supplement called 'Culture', where it is largely the Arnoldian meaning that is intended. These pages deal with theatre, art, books, music, cinema and so on. Arnold might well be shocked at some of the contents of the films or the admission of 'pop' music into this section, but he would at least recognize the field. Thus in everyday usage 'culture' retains its creative or aesthetic meaning, even if the term has enlarged its territory of significance in ways that Arnold did not foresee and might not approve.

Especially during the first half of the twentieth century, anthropologists and sociologists developed Tylor's approach and gave 'culture' a much wider meaning, so that it became almost synonymous with a way of life, and less associated with the worlds of thought or art. People speak of a 'culture of self-development' or even a 'culture of violence'. In a recent radio interview I noted criticism of a 'political culture of bribery'. Clearly this second set of meanings would not fit into that Sunday cultural supplement: it points instead to a cluster of assumptions about what is acceptable within a certain context. As Archbishop Derek Worlock once put it, with Liverpool-style bluntness, culture is simply 'the way we do things around here'.[5] Whatever is the 'done thing' can still dominate within more cohesive cultures, but as soon as people move away from the confines of home or traditional settings, they discover that there is more than one way of doing things: at this point an awareness of cultural diversity makes everything seem more complex and can dramatically change the agenda of religious adherence and religious belonging.

One recalls the famous remark of Goering that when he heard the word culture he wanted to reach for his gun. He probably had the more elite meaning in mind – the world of art or ideas. If he experienced today's extension of 'culture' and the diversification of 'cultures', he might well reach for a heavier weapon. And yet the word seems here to stay. Whatever the niceties of vocabulary or emphasis, it is now a part of our general 'culture' to realize that 'culture' constitutes a total context that shapes us all, and this stress on the hidden power of culture goes beyond the more descriptive stance of both Arnold and Tylor. The Arnold emphasis dealt with what can be called 'objective' or 'conscious' culture, highlighting such cultural products as art and institutions. The Tylor approach focused more on 'subjective' or 'invisible' culture, including all the modes of meaning and perception that people assimilate within a society. Later in these pages we shall see that the supremacy of these two schools of thinking about culture has been challenged in recent decades by more explanatory, penetrating and socio-political questions. Do we construct culture or does culture construct us? What is the process of production behind the accepted forms and practices of culture? Who controls the vehicles of cultural formation? How can we participate in the creation of culture? But for the moment we concentrate on mainstream approaches to the description of culture.

Six categories

Initial help in this task can be had from a now famous book of 1952, which listed some 164 definitions of culture, categorizing them into six major groups and further sub-groups.[6] That exercise in clarification remains extremely useful but it needs adaptation to include the many new emphases of the last forty years. I propose here to summarize that classic work of Kroeber and Kluckhohn, to review some key contributions of more recent decades, and then to outline an updated model for understanding the diversity of meaning of 'culture' today, keeping in mind the scope of these pages – the relation of culture to faith and of faith to culture.

Six principal categories of definitions of culture were identified by Kroeber and Kluckhohn.

1.   The first kind consists of *descriptive* accounts of culture, which seek to list the key elements that make up the *'complex whole'* that is culture. Indeed that phrase, as already seen, was first used by Edward Tylor in 1871 and was repeated in their respective definitions of culture by Ruth Benedict in 1929 and by Margaret Mead in 1937. Hence the first key to understanding culture is its non-simplicity: it refers to a coming together of different elements such as meanings, values, symbols, beliefs, practices and so on. Some thinkers will question the emphasis on unity or a 'whole', insisting that culture study is often tempted to find patterns of coherence at the expense of the inevitable pluralism within a culture; but practically nobody disagrees as to the converging complex that is culture.

2.   A second ingredient in definitions of culture is some *historical dimension*, in the sense that culture is received as a 'social heritage' from the past, and thus is communicated from one generation to another.

3.   Thirdly, a culture is viewed as involving a particular set of assumptions about values and behaviour, and hence it contains certain *normative elements* that influence the life of a group. Some experts here introduce a distinction between 'culture' as referring to the way of life of all groups, and 'a culture' as pointing to the specific modes of behaviour that are accepted in a given society.

4.   Fourthly, some definitions deal with the *psychological functions* served by culture, for instance in creating security through traditional responses to such great human issues as sexuality or death, or as answering the need for social order through systems of law or organization. Thus culture has a formative role where people learn how to cope with life in ways that have been tested in the past. It provides a *philosophy* or a *cosmology* to answer some of the fundamental questions about life.

5. Fifthly, culture provides a *structure* for living together, both a structure of meaning and an inherited way of organizing relations between people. Some cultures will be more rooted in authority and others favour looser forms of cohesion and belonging, but some structuring of social life is a constant across different forms of culture.

6. Sixthly, some approaches tackle the question of the *genesis* of culture, and these tend to stress that culture is not simply an automatic inheritance between generations but a conscious human product, born of different forms of human association. In the words of Clyde Kluckhohn, 'culture designates those aspects of the total human environment, tangible and intangible, that have been created' by human beings themselves.[7] In so far as culture is therefore a human product, some authors highlight the fact that humans are symbol-using animals and hence that symbols rather than concepts are the natural vehicles for mediating the meanings and values embodied in cultures.

Before trying to offer a somewhat different synthesis of essential elements for understanding of culture – one that can serve the more specifically religious purposes of this book – it may be useful to see how these six elements are either present or absent in a few more recent accounts of culture. From a vast field I single out three English-language approaches because of their diversity from one another, and also because they highlight aspects partially neglected in the summary of Kroeber and Kluckhohn.

Geertz, Lonergan and Williams

According to a widely quoted definition offered by Clifford Geertz, culture 'denotes an historically transmitted pattern of meanings embodied in symbols, a system of inherited conceptions expressed in symbolic forms by means of which men communicate, perpetuate, and develop their knowledge about and attitudes toward life'.[8] In his own words, he espouses a 'semiotic' concept of culture, in the sense that he seeks to study the sign systems underlying human behaviour. He compares culture to 'webs of significance' that humanity has spun, and any analysis of culture will try to understand the complex meaning embodied in those social and symbolic webs.[9] By coincidence, the Latin for 'web' is *textum*, and some more recent thinkers like to speak about 'culture texts': 'a text can be a set of words, an event, or even a person. Culture then becomes the total sum of these texts shared by a given people'.[10]

Geertz, unlike most of the authors cited by Kroeber and Kluck-hohn, gives prominence to the crucial role of symbols as carriers of culture, and this aspect seems of special relevance in reflecting on the relations of culture and religious faith. By placing symbolic communication at the core of his definition, he is also seeking to do justice to the 'informal logic of actual life', holding that 'society's forms are culture's substance'.[11] Apart from this new priority of symbols, in fact his definition touches on four of the six key elements mentioned above: historical transmission (no. 2), more philo-sophical-psychological dimensions (no. 4), culture as a context that provides 'control mechanisms'[12] (no. 5) and which embodies itself in symbolic forms (no. 6). Interestingly, in this short definition, Geertz does not suggest anything about the 'complex whole' that culture entails; at one point he speaks of an 'accumulated totality',[13] but generally he is more aware of the diversity of culture than of its unity. He has moved away from the older 'functionalist' approach, which highlighted how elements in a culture interrelate and have different purposes in creating social cohesion. This functionalist school, in fact, had tended to neglect the symbolic wavelength of culture.

In a later book Geertz broadens the agenda to include 'common sense' as 'an everywhere-found cultural form' of a less tightly in-tegrated kind, expressed in the 'of-courseness' of different cultures.[14] This links up with the emphasis on hidden assumptions that was discussed in the introductory chapter here. Lived culture is practically identical with the common sense of a society, and as such can be a major obstacle or ally for religious faith. Geertz sums up the omnipresence of this cultural system in an eloquent passage:

> Religion rests its case on revelation, science on method, ideology on moral passion; but common sense rests its on the assertion that it is not a case at all, just life in a nutshell. The world is its authority.[15]

In fact the Canadian theologian Bernard Lonergan, who was mentioned briefly in the introduction, also studied common sense as a gathering of incomplete insights that remain 'within the familiar world of things'; the level of common sense 'discourages the effort to understand', and this in-built 'bias of common sense' can be an element of lived culture that undermines authentic culture.[16] Lonergan in different decades of his writing offers somewhat different accounts of culture, one more general and the other more historical:

> Man can pause and with a smile or a forced grin ask what the drama, what he himself is about. His culture is his capacity to ask, to reflect, to reach an answer that at once satisfies his intelligence and speaks to his heart.[17]

> The contemporary notion of culture is empirical. A culture is a set of meanings and values informing a common way of life, and there are as many cultures as there are distinct sets of such meanings and values. However, this manner of conceiving culture is relatively recent. It is the product of empirical human studies. Within less than one hundred years it has replaced an older, classicist view that had flourished for over two millennia. On the older view culture was conceived not empirically but normatively. It was the opposite of barbarism . . . It stressed not facts but values. It could not but claim to be universalist.[18]

With the term 'informing', used in the sense of giving form to (rather than modern 'information'), Lonergan bridges the inner world of philosophies and the outer world of shared patterns of life, and in his own way touches on practically all the six elements highlighted by Kroeber and Kluckhohn. For him, however, it is not enough to identify culture with what (as we shall see) Raymond Williams calls a 'whole way of life': Lonergan prefers to see culture as the communal expression of our self-understanding – through art, language and through the visions implicit in how we live and act. In his words, 'culture is the meaning of a way of life' and thus he proposes a distinction between the social and the cultural, akin to the old relationship of body and soul.[19]

If one accepts Lonergan's philosophical emphasis, the social realm is more visible and more vast, whereas the more restricted field of culture is immanent behind the appearances of society. In this sense culture is sometimes spoken of as a 'superstructure', above the merely sociological, and at other times as 'underlying' the externals of society. Although the metaphors may seem to conflict, in fact they point in the same direction, to a view of culture as a more internal and intentional horizon of human consciousness than social organization and behaviour. However useful such a distinction may be, it should not be made too absolute because these spheres are inevitably connected in practice. In this perspective culture is in perpetual dialogue between two dimensions, one more invisible and one more visible. We can describe the complex patterns of a 'way of life' – that is the first level of anthropology; but we need also to inquire further into the underlying world-views 'informing' that more external realm of shared life. Culture involves, therefore, the interaction of two dimensions: more hidden sets of assumptions (meanings and values) and the more manifest field of observable social patterns (common ways of life).

The view of culture proposed by the British writer Raymond Williams has some parallels to Lonergan, although they were not aware of each other's writings. At times Williams seems remarkably close to the words of the Canadian theologian: thus in 1961 he wrote of the analysis of culture as entailing 'the clarification of the meanings and values implicit and explicit in a particular way of life'.[20] He went on to describe the culture of any given period as a 'structure of feeling', born from a process of 'interaction between patterns learned and created in the mind and patterns communicated and made active in relationships, conventions and institutions'.[21]

Apart from being Professor of Drama at Cambridge University, he had a life-long passion for researching the changing culture of recent centuries. In his view the evolution of the idea of culture mirrors our responses to the huge changes in social conditions and in human relationships since the industrial revolution. As early as 1958 he summarized the story of the term 'culture' as follows:

> . . . it had meant, primarily, the 'tending of natural growth', and then, by analogy, a process of human training. But this

latter use, which had usually been a culture *of* something, was changed, in the nineteenth century, to *culture* as such, a thing in itself. It came to mean, first, 'a general state or habit of the mind', having close relations with the ideal of human perfection. Second, it came to mean 'the general state of intellectual development, in a society as a whole'. Third, it came to mean 'the general body of the arts'. Fourth, later in the century, it came to mean 'a whole way of life, material, intellectual and spiritual'.[22]

In a more personal essay of that same year he wrote that 'Culture is ordinary: that is the first fact', in the sense that every society has its own purposes and meanings which it embodies in 'a whole way of life'.[23] In a later book he traces the shift in meaning of 'culture' from the 'active cultivation' of the mind to a 'configuration' of the spirit of a people in the eighteenth century. In the next century anthropology stressed the plural nature of culture as pointing to distinctive ways of life. Later still came a more 'materialist' sense of culture as a direct or indirect 'product' of 'cultural practice' within a given social order.[24] From this materialist point of view, shifts in sensibility are nearly always linked to changes in economic systems and work patterns which in turn influence life-styles.

As well as being a historian Williams was a socialist who liked to stress particular cultures as products of specific social situations. At times he seems to accept the interpretation of culture as primarily a way of life: 'a culture is not only a body of intellectual and imaginative work; it is also and essentially a whole way of life'.[25] But often he wants to go beyond this descriptive approach, expressing a certain impatience with the neutrality and even innocence of definitions which do not 'make room for study of manifestly signifying institutions, practices and works'.[26] To do justice to the complex realities of modern societies it is necessary to see culture as a *product* of definite forces at work in history and to inquire how it is *embedded* in a whole range of activities. Hence Williams prefers to define culture as 'the signifying system through which . . . a social order is communicated, reproduced, experienced, and explored'.[27] One could say that Williams is making his own fusion of three of the six elements of Kroeber and Kluckhohn as listed earlier (the normative, structural and genetic approaches to culture), but with his more politically alert philosophy, he seeks to question the whole set of 'practices' implicit in any culture, asking in particular about 'the means of cultural production'[28] – the influences behind the particular features of a dominant culture.

It is worth adding that the French philosopher and sociologist Pierre Bourdieu echoes Raymond Williams' emphasis on 'practices' as the key to understanding culture but he gives pride of place to what he calls 'habitus': by this he means a system of ever-changing 'mental dispositions' underlying the 'values which dominate the whole of our experience'. Deeply linked with language – that central but elusive carrier of cultural attitudes – the 'habitus' is shaped through all the agents that have an impact on an individual, from parents to education to the symbolic power of institutions and social hierarchies.[29] Once again we are forced to recognize the doubleness of culture: it involves observable practices or socially legitimated ways of acting but it also entails a more concealed set of subjective attitudes often assimilated unconsciously over a long time. Together these habits of acting and of interpreting can either imprison people within prejudices or they can become avenues towards authentic living, towards self-transcending choices that challenge the negative bias of any culture.

Towards a synthesis

Faced with this diversity of approach to culture, one becomes aware of significant tensions between one emphasis and another. For the sake of simplicity, one could suggest three main schools among the several tendencies just mentioned: the *neutral* description of culture as a convergence of various elements in human society and history; the *idealist* tendency to highlight meanings, ideas, symbols, and (perhaps but not always) values; a more *political and moral* sense of culture as conditioning human choices and actions and therefore as having often unconscious power over human behaviour. Thus variations on Tylor and Arnold continue but their monopoly is now challenged by a third approach that insists that culture is as an ambiguous *product*: this stresses that since culture is a human construct involving many conflicting values, cultural analysis needs to focus on how it is produced as well as on how it can be transformed.

In the light of the multi-faceted nature of culture, one can appreciate the rich synthesis offered by the UNESCO definition, which is the product of an international conference on 'Cultural Policies', held in Mexico in 1982. This complex statement seeks to do justice both to the 'creative' or conscious culture exemplified by the imaginative, intellectual and spiritual dimensions of life, and to the more 'lived' sense of culture associated with anthropology and sociology:

> Culture may now be said to be the whole complex of distinctive spiritual, material, intellectual and emotional features that characterize a society or social group. It includes not only the arts and letters, but also modes of life, the fundamental rights of the human being, value systems, traditions and beliefs . . . It is culture that gives man the ability to reflect upon himself. It is culture that makes us specifically human, rational beings, endowed with a critical judgment and a sense of moral commitment. It is through culture that we discern values and make choices. It is through culture that man expresses himself, becomes aware of himself, recognizes his incompleteness, questions his own achievements, seeks untiringly for new meanings and creates works through which he transcends his limitations.[30]

This remarkable gathering of insights begins by echoing the 'complex whole' expression of Edward Tylor. Of the remaining five dimensions of culture, as mentioned above, the UNESCO account is strangely silent on the historical process of communicating human vision across generations, but it includes in one way or another all the other four aspects: normative 'value systems'; psychological and philosophical quest for 'new meanings'; the 'material' structures of a 'tradition'; and this text is quite eloquent about culture as productive and active in its exploration of human experience. In this way it takes the more anthropological question about the 'genesis' of culture and enlarges it to cover the whole adventure of 'spiritual' awareness and of how a human being 'transcends' the limits of his or her situation. It is worth noting that these two words ('spiritual' and 'transcends') are the first and last key words of this whole statement, thus leaving it much more open to the religious horizon than any of the more academic descriptions of culture cited earlier in this chapter.

In the light of all this, we can attempt a synthesis of the multi-dimensional nature of culture, especially with the central concern of this book in mind – the interaction of culture and Christian faith in today's context. From what has already been seen, what aspects appear essential for any description of 'culture'?

1.   It is a uniquely human creation or product, a horizon that distinguishes human beings from animals. As such it is an embodiment of human freedom and transcendence.

2.   It is something inherited from the past, and yet it changes and adapts in order to cope with different moments of history and different environments.

3.   It evolves into a selective set of assumptions, often unconsciously assimilated within a given group or society. Thus culture has an enormous impact on the quality and tone of religious faith.

4.   Culture involves an entire way of life shared by people; as such it is a source of solidarity and identity.

5.   Underlying this social manifestation culture is found to involve a 'whole complex' or convergence of visible factors and acquired ways of interpreting the world.

6.   For instance, culture carries and expresses:
     (a) meanings and beliefs (or visions of life);
     (b) values (norms for behaviour);
     (c) customs, practices and traditions (patterns of response).

7.   Cultural expressions may frequently embody themselves in institutions and systems (which preserve those meanings and values) or in symbolic forms (a handshake, a flag, a ritual, etc.).

8.   The field of culture ranges from everyday routines and responses to larger explorations of the significance and worth of existence. Indeed different layers often converge in one simple act: eating together serves both nutrition and a sense of belonging.[31]

9.   At its 'higher' reaches, culture includes not only such spiritual activities as art or literature, but some ultimately religious vision.

10.   By its nature, culture is self-communicating, seeking to pass on its cumulative wisdom to future generations; in this respect it runs into difficulty during periods of rapid change of social forms.

11.   Since they are historical products, shaped by complex political influences, cultures are fallible constructs, in need of constant discernment, questioning and renewal.

12.   Throughout most of human history, cultures have been rooted in religious consciousness; a central crisis of culture today comes from the split between culture and religion over the last two centuries or so.

That last horizon points towards the next few chapters here, which will deal with the increasing attention to culture by Christian churches today.

Chapter Two

Three Theorists of Change

> *[What is] dubious is the general nineteenth century presumption that modernity adversely affects religion by taking the wonder and mystery out of the universe – as if religion depends more on the physical environment than on the quality of social relations.*
>
> (Mary Douglas)[1]

> *Technology, like anything else new, must be faced not in a spirit of nostalgia but in the historical spirit. A kind of cosmic nostalgia, the desire somehow to escape from history, is an old pagan disease. There is nothing Christian in it.* (Walter J. Ong)[2]

This chapter offers the reader a synopsis of insights from three stimulating thinkers. All happen to be Catholics but only occasionally do they comment explicitly on religious issues. However, their secular fields of specialization provide interestingly different approaches to cultural change.

Social contexts for culture

Mary Douglas is a contemporary cultural anthropologist, who did most of her initial field-work in Africa in the 1950s, and particularly in Zaire. Author of many books, she has consistently criticized some common assumptions of sociologists on such issues as secularization of the pre-modern world. Thus in the best-known study of her earlier years, *Natural Symbols: Explorations in Cosmology*, she argues that the contrast of secular with religious has nothing to do with the contrast of modern with traditional: in her judgement the idea that primitive people are by nature religious is untenable. Instead all kinds of 'scepticism, materialism and spiritual fervour are to be found in the range of tribal societies'.[3] Therefore she casts doubt on the thesis that secularism – in the sense of a this-worldly framework that remains within everyday concerns – is mainly a product of urbanization or of the rise of science, or the breakdown of traditional social cohesion. Instead it is 'an age-old cosmological type, a product of a definable social experience'.[4]

Differences between cultures, according to Douglas, are rooted in how people learn to perceive their social relationships with one another. In this regard four factors are mutually reinforcing: the acquired ways of perceiving one's place in society, the social context and its dominant patterns of interaction, individual behaviour choices, and the forms of religious vision typical of different cultures. A child starts by assimilating the social assumptions of the 'tribe', and gradually the self comes to view the surrounding world with a particular slant, which in turn shapes his or her typical expectations of others. Thus people live certain implicit choices and these form a shared common sense that seems natural but in fact is a product of a certain way of being together. The tone and quality of these relationships in turn influence the kind of religious horizon likely within a given culture. Douglas insists on a cultural analysis that gives pride of place to the individual's way of responding to the surrounding world, but in addition she stresses the connection between these different perceptions of the self in society with various forms of religious or non-religious visions of existence. How the individual experiences these interactions involves an implicit choice concerning what Douglas calls a cosmology.

She is especially known for her four models of cultural difference and of how the variations between different social contexts and cosmologies can be understood in terms of what she calls 'grid' and 'group'. This is a flexible but simple way of describing how people live with different built-in interpretative schemes of how to act in relation to others. It provides a method of categorizing cultural differences and cultural change. It also helps to show how cultural categories, far from being autonomous from social relationships, are always influenced by social situations. Culture and society in this presentation can never be divorced, nor can one of them dominate the other totally. Here I shall seek to explain the four-fold typology of cultures in order to suggest how this model casts light on the contemporary situation of culture and faith.

'Group' refers to forms of authority and the pressure on the individual exercised by a closed society: allegiance to the group leadership is central. Where 'group' is strong, conformity and obedience are key influences, and people tend to be classified as members or not, as either insiders or outsiders.

'Grid' refers to a less controlling and less explicit form of organization, constituted by the network of roles, rules and relationships that people build up with one another. 'Grid' is both more informal and more complex than 'group', focusing on the self rather than on the collectivity. Hence 'grid' is less a question of social control from above than of assumptions that guide how individuals behave to one another in different situations. By putting the two wavelengths of social organization together, Douglas shows how society can move from highly structured to highly unstructured situations, not only in terms of social obedience (group) but also in terms of interpersonal expectations (grid). She advances the thesis that the resulting four forms of organization (with all kinds of inner nuances depending on the position on a graph) are at the root of how cultural forms have an influence on religion. In her words there is a 'dependence of the form of religion on the form of organization'.[5] As in her own presentations of this group-grid theory, it is best understood with the aid of a diagram.

The vertical line represents the range of 'grid' influence, from zero presence at the bottom to strongest at the top. Similarly the horizontal line represents the range of 'group' control, from zero at the left to strongest at the right. In this way four squares emerge from the different possible combinations of grid and group, thus offering a flexible model for identifying four quite different cultural formations. As Douglas has written, 'culture is nothing if not a collective product',[6] and she approaches it through the different patterns or fields of relationships that make up a community.

Starting with the top right square – position 'A' – one has what could be called traditional culture, where both grid and group are strong. Such a culture involves a combination of clear authority, a hierarchy that commands group life, with a network of implicit norms that structure interaction between individuals. Stability and dependency are features of such a culture. Religiously there is usually a strong sense of divine transcendence, celebrated through set rituals, and further reinforced through fear of divine punishment

TYPES OF CULTURES

GRID
strong = network of assumptions/rules
guiding behaviour of individuals,
shared social expectations

'B'
self at centre,
competitive individualism,
market-exchange relationships,
materialist symbols of status

'A'
order/balance of hierarchical
society,
sense of belonging + stable
relationships with others

GROUP
weak

GROUP
strong = allegiance,
control,
conformity,
pressure on individuals

'C'
isolated individuals,
no structures, supports or
fixed roles,
transitory relations,
secularist horizon

'D'
'sect'-style collectivity,
authoritarian regime,
fundamentalism,
strict separation of
insiders/outsiders

GRID
weak

for any transgression against loyalty to the community (group) or against the accepted rules that govern interpersonal behaviour (grid). It has been argued that the typical 'Catholic culture' of the decades before Vatican II was of this tightly ordered kind.[7] There is no need to interpret this 'A' square as automatically a domineering or unhappy culture. In fact within this square there can be flexible and humane forms of authority and secure social roles: when this happens, this culture offers a set of supports for the individual that most people are looking for, even today. It is the natural culture that throughout the ages has provided a home for human beings and given them a religious cosmology with which to confront the dilemmas of existence.

The shift from the top right to the top left-hand square is one way of understanding the major cultural movement that leads from a stable culture where religion is part of the fabric of life to a more free-floating and individualist culture where the language of religion undergoes severe challenge. In the understanding of Mary Douglas, a culture without 'group' allegiance but with high 'grid' interaction is essentially a competitive society rooted in exchange relationships of a quasi-commercial kind. The sense of belonging to a definite group is lessened but 'ego-centred categories of behaviour' are at a maximum.[8] Role definition does not come any longer from some collective authority but rather from gaining recognition in a competitive market with other individuals. The appearance of success becomes important, and one is reminded of the conflict at the heart of Jane Austen's novels, between a traditional ethic of objective virtue and the more subjectivist behaviour that Austen satirizes as connected with city life.

As loyalty to the group diminishes, a more individualist status-seeking becomes central: the curbs on this more ego-based culture that were present in Square 'A' lessen dramatically in Square 'B', simply because individual interaction ('grid') now monopolizes the field, without the balancing influence of social responsibility ('group'). Relationships and alliances become fragile and temporary. With a decline of group identity and of a sense of belonging, a culture becomes more pluralistic, more pragmatic and more materialist in its symbols of success. Self-interest is a principal driving force behind individual choices and behaviour. In such a culture even religious forms become more ego-based. God is less a revelation to be obeyed than a source of peace and comfort for the self. Thus, in what Douglas describes as 'a distinctive culture of competitive individualism', the tendency is to foster 'personal religion'.[9] Typical of this context is that religion is privatized and called upon to meet people's needs for self-fulfilment. This inevitably entails a certain secularization of religion, even if a fuller form of secularism is more likely to be found in Square 'C'.

It is not hard to recognize many aspects of urban 'modernity' in what Douglas describes as low-group and strong-grid, but her analysis puts the emphasis less on the external situation of a city than on the changing place of the self within the social organization. When one moves to the bottom left square, one finds a more extreme (perhaps 'Postmodern') lack of structures and supports. Here role definition is at a minimum, since there are pressures from neither the 'group' nor the 'grid'. Relationships become even more optional and mobile. Whereas in 'B' there was a certain community of competition, in 'C' isolation and lack of communication between people are typical features. Everything is floating, as exemplified in 'modern industrial society [where] there are probably more opportunities to live as an isolate than ever'.[10] She cites the example of a girl working at a cash checkpoint in a supermarket as a summary of this culture of minimum grid and minimum group pressures: within the patterns of such a job there is practically no opportunity to relate to people or to have any sense of belonging.

From the point of view of religion, if a certain reductiveness of faith to individual needs was characteristic of 'B', in 'C' secularist indifference becomes dominant. If the main form of unbelief in 'A' is an opting out of the structures of belonging (for instance, from Church practice), and if in 'B' the tendency is to reject God as irrelevant to my life, in 'C' the very question of some ultimate meaning and spiritual horizon fades into silence or unreality. The first impression of this Square of structureless existence is that it is a disaster area for Christian faith, where the sense of wonder shrivels up and there is no longer any language for speaking of the mystery of God. However, at least one religious commentator offers a much more positive reading of this cultural situation: it is so lacking in structures that it is free to build 'intentional Christian communities' creatively and from below. This interpretation assumes that the very absence of control from group or grid is a cultural blessing, where personal identity will come 'from an awareness of one's self-worth and potential for change', and hence it provides fertile ground for counter-cultural communities to grow.[11]

This may be true for some people, but on average this empty space seems more likely to lead to a certain cultural desolation, where drifting dominates and where lack of supports leaves people without any scaffolding for an encounter with religious revelation. Moreover, insofar as today's cultural situation in much of the

Western world leaves people isolated along the line of the 'C' Square, a frequent result seems to be an anchorless form of spiritual searching of the New Age variety. The absence of pressures may provoke creative freedom and rediscovery of the gospel for some, but a more probable outcome – one that is increasingly verified in the comfortable post-industrial world – is a return of gnostic credulity without any contact with the traditional wisdom of the Churches. In other words, without some belonging to a 'group' or some community links with the 'grid' of other people, the typical cultural form of religiousness can easily become secularized, unchurched, narcissistic and lonely.

Square 'D' represents a radically different response to the complexity of today, the conservative tendency to close the doors of dialogue between faith and culture, a stance of distance and of negative judgement against the dominant values around, and ultimately a return of religious fundamentalism. Douglas would not necessarily agree with giving labels to the previous three squares: nevertheless, 'A' is largely premodern, 'B' summarizes many ills of modernity, and 'C' seems to include many of the elements of the 'postmodern'. If so, then 'D' represents the reaction on behalf of various religious groups today to withdraw into highly structured fortresses of resistance to the chaos that they perceive in late modernity and postmodernity.

In studying the 'weak grid/strong group' form of culture, which Douglas has on different occasions called the 'enclave' or the 'sect' model, she stresses the desire to insulate the tight group from the surrounding world and the low priority given to horizontal relationships between people ('grid'). Allegiance to authority is all, and is often accompanied by a rigid asceticism concerning pleasure or non-conformity of any kind. Such a situation of dependency is one into which a new-born baby always comes, but when imposed on adults it entails a danger of authoritarianism that discourages any individual creativity or freedom.

Dramatic and extreme examples of this 'D' culture are provided by the various tragedies involving religious sects in recent years: the suicide-massacres in different countries or the sect behind the bombing of the Tokyo underground. But Douglas would see this cultural form embodied in any situation where collectivism outweighs individual choices and imposes various roles on its members. This kind of group often presents itself to itself as egalitarian but in reality this entails an absence of scope for individual initiative. Another self-image is as a dissenting minority and this goes hand in hand with a certain suspicion towards non-members. As Douglas remarks concerning all types of culture, 'Paradoxically the greatest source of strength for entrenching a particular cultural bias is the mutual hostility between cultures'.[12] This comment seems particularly true for the preservation of group identity in this sectarian form of culture.

Standing back from the details of this fourfold diagram, one should stress that it is a question of understanding the silent pressures of different cultural contexts on the individual and hence on the possibility of arriving at religious commitment. In the words of Mary Douglas, 'Decisions are difficult to reach. They rest on tacit assumptions, not on argued syllogisms.' And she adds that the social organization that comes to seem natural in different cultures constitutes a particular 'path' of decision making for the members of that culture. 'This is the central argument of cultural theory: culture itself is constrained' by its own 'different logical base' and this can help to explain 'how any type of collective can resist pressures to transform'.[13] The great advantage of her grid/group model is to have clarified different forms of base and bias in diverse cultures, of their mutual resistance and conflict, and of their divergent assumptions and priorities. She shows how underlying visions and beliefs, rooted in various forms of social expectation and control, produce four completely different forms of culture. Although she identified these conflicting forms of cultural environment in 'primitive' tribes, her insights are of considerable relevance for understanding our present cultural shifts and indeed the misunderstandings that can arise between different sub-cultures within Christianity today.

The issue of cultural agency

More briefly, and by way of contrast to Mary Douglas, we can draw upon another British expert on the interaction of society and culture. The sociologist Margaret Archer starts from the everyday experience of how people feel both imprisoned by and yet able to resist the socio-cultural pressures surrounding them. Her goal is to describe how cultural transformation may come about. First of all, however, she rejects any image of culture as a neatly coherent ethos or 'symbolically consistent universe'; instead of being such an all-inclusive web, culture is a 'shapeless, seething and shifting thing'.[14] Her analysis of this mobility within culture is grounded in a distinction between a 'Cultural System' and the 'Socio-cultural' domain. Archer practically identifies the system of culture with the 'ideas' component that holds sway within any given society (and hence is loosely parallel to 'group' for Douglas). By contrast, the socio-cultural structure has to do with lived interactions between people (and partly similar to 'grid'). In Archer's view, whenever one finds 'high Socio-Cultural integration' as a way of life, this is more crucial than any impositions of a cultural belief system: 'culture is *not* always shared because it is binding but may sometimes be *binding because shared*'.[15]

Clearly, therefore, it would be wrong to present Archer as simply echoing Douglas. Her theory of change (or 'morphogenesis') involves a complicated analysis of possible ways in which 'culture' and 'structure' can influence one another. 'Culture', in the sense of the beliefs that dominate a society, can be either static or in ferment. 'Structure', in the sense of interest groups that hold power, can also be firmly established or else in conflict. Hence, if 'ideational control' goes hand in hand with unchallenged structural domination one has a very traditionalist society (a case of 'structural morphostasis and cultural morphostasis').[16] But this is not often the case in the contemporary world. Sometimes the push for transformation begins on the level of 'culture' and sometimes on the level of 'structure'. Thus the Enlightenment started on the level of ideas and then had an impact on the political shape of society. Similarly, the Scientific Revolution was initially intellectual; the Industrial Revolution (born indirectly from the new sciences) was more a social phenomenon influencing work patterns and causing rapid urbanization. In this way material or economic innovations can initiate a series of social changes, which only later result in upsetting cultural stability and throwing long-accepted meanings for life into crisis.

Margaret Archer insists that her theory of change is not an

endorsement of cultural determinism. Cultural systems of value and meaning come into existence as a result of historical interactions on the social level, and the system can then seem to have a life of its own – imposing constraints on people but also offering new openings. In spite of the inevitable limitations of any culture – due to place, language, education and so on – Archer wants to stress that a different future can be forged through forms of cultural 'agency', as a result of the 'reflective ability of human beings to fight back against their conditioning'.[17] Even from this brief account of some of her insights, it is clear that she offers not just analytical models of change but a powerful argument that although cultural transformation is highly complex, it is still possible to counteract the dominant culture and to help create alternative forms of culture.

Walter Ong: oral vs *print cultures*

The work of Walter J. Ong offers a complementary perspective for these insights from anthropology and sociology. The background of this American Jesuit lies in literary criticism and in theology and his special field of interest over many years is the significance of the shifts in our ways of human communication – moving from oral cultures to the writing and printing revolutions and then to the electronic media of today. These three major evolutions were brought about by technological developments, and in each case the arrival of new technology had a major impact on culture itself. When, for instance, writing ousted the patterns of an older oral culture, it 'transformed human consciousness', introducing 'division and alienation' but also 'highly interiorized stages of consciousness'.[18] Then a different phase of thinking arrived, when printing allowed knowledge to be localized in visual space, as distinct from the essentially communal and present-tense communication typical of 'orality'. The eye took over from the ear as the chief contact with reality. Thus writing and printing located knowledge in space, with the cold objectivity of words on a page. Oral cultures had trusted more in the temporal world of speech and were therefore more naturally community-based.

Moreover, all these cultural developments presented challenges for the mediation of religious faith. Whereas sound is 'related to present actuality rather than to past or future', and is 'a special sensory key to interiority',[19] the new dominance of the visual caused a depersonalization of culture and indeed a privatization of religion. From a theological point of view, Ong is a great defender of the human values of 'orality', without ever falling into the nostalgia of regretting subsequent cultural wavelengths (or idealizing a less literate past). Faith comes from hearing, according to St Paul. In Ong's view the sound of the spoken word is an avenue into the interior of the other person. Printed communication is much more distant and impersonal by comparison. Indeed the 'decay of dialogue', that was one of the indirect effects of the invention of the printing press, constituted a radically different context for the communication of faith. Print makes reality private and seemingly controllable whereas 'the spoken word moves from interior to interior' and genuine inter-personal encounter is 'achieved largely through voice'.[20]

What Mary Douglas saw in the shift from more traditional to more individualist societies, Walter Ong associated with the visualization of reality caused by the cultural revolution inaugurated by the technology of writing and of its later developments – book culture and printing. 'Writing seals off its product from direct dialogue: the writer creates his text in isolation'; as in the case of Douglas' interpretation of the move into 'B', a certain lonely individualism results.[21] When human communication loses its quality of encounter and of direct relationship, thinking itself undergoes a subtle change and human consciousness is restructured in its sense of the real. When a print mentality dominates, we tend to desire 'closure' or certitude of a visible and verifiable kind. In this cultural situation, the truth of religious revelation can be dismissed as insufficiently objective and its nature as a relational and spoken Word remain neglected. In this sense print culture is one of the gateways to the empirical science that seemed the only conceivable kind during modernity.

What Ong calls 'oral-aural' culture (because it involves both a speaking and a listening) is much more existentially real than the strange act of reading in silence. When he turns his attention to the twentieth century, Ong becomes enthusiastic about the potentials of a 'secondary orality', caused by yet another technological development that again is having enormous impact on human consciousness: the world of electronic communications – especially radio and television – has retrieved the lost dimension of voice. This development is capable of healing some of the cultural imbalances caused by the impersonal world of print. It is not a question of returning to the 'primary orality' of preliterate cultures but of a new contact with personal interiority and mystery, and hence with the question of God. What printed visualization tended to neglect, this new orality makes possible again. Its relational quality not only leaves room for faith but fosters the human capacities for interpersonal hearing where the Word can enter. Thus as distinct from the 'closed fields of systems' of print, now there is a fresh openness 'connected with our new kind of orality, the secondary orality of our electronic age'.[22] The new culture is fascinated with interconnections and with personal interiority. It values diversity and convergence thinking. It repersonalizes the world that printing had made reductively 'spatial'. This second orality also values the present moment whereas writing tends to remove life from time.

In Ong's view of cultural history, offered here in a necessarily compressed form, the arrival of writing and of printing marks a crucial dividing line in history. He sees its overall impact as questionable and ambiguous, especially during the period of modernity. But if we are integrating orality into culture again, an excessive focus on private and visual reading may give way to a more interpersonal sense of encounter. This will be one of the many strands of postmodernity and of its possibly greater openness to the religious dimension.

Chapter Three

A Major Theme of Vatican II

The meaning of Vatican II was the acknowledgement of history.
(Bernard Lonergan)[1]

The central non-ecclesiological issue at the Second Vatican Council and in the Post-Conciliar Church is the relationship between faith and culture. (Dermot Lane)[2]

The Second Vatican Council initiated a whole new wavelength for Roman Catholic understanding of culture. It was the first time in Church history that an ecumenical council debated at length on such an issue and then devoted a substantial chapter to this theme in *Gaudium et Spes*, the Pastoral Constitution dealing with the Church in the Modern World. Although this chapter was considerably longer than the three sections dealing with atheism, in the years immediately after the Council, great attention was given to the issue of atheism, and only gradually – from the mid-seventies onwards – have cultural concerns come to the centre of the stage. In this chapter the aim is to outline the significance of the Vatican II stance on culture; the one following will examine later developments in Catholic thinking in this area.

The story of the surprising birth of *Gaudium et Spes* has often been told, and needs only a brief summary here. It was an unexpected child of the Council: at the outset the proposed texts, prepared by the Roman Curia, remained within the mould of an old-fashioned theology – defensive, neo-scholastic and ahistorical. Moreover, the topics were all 'ad intra', dealing with ecclesial issues such as liturgy or the Church's sense of its own identity. At an early stage of the three-year period of the Council, the Bishops voted to jettison the prepared drafts and to start their reflections from a significantly different basis. This was an indication of the minor revolution that marked the Council, which embodied itself in two new priorities:

opting for a return to the roots of revelation as a source of renewal, and for a more positive listening to the situations of today as 'signs of the times'. Such a stance, combining spiritual and pastoral approaches, ousted the entrenched attitudes of intellectualism and negative judgements against modern culture.

In the early sessions of the Council there was practically no attention to the 'modern world' in itself, and it was only when the Council had been underway for more than a year that the proposal was made to devote time and effort to discerning today's context for faith, the world 'ad extra', beyond the confines of Church. From this initiative *Gaudium et Spes* came into being – a long document that can be viewed as an essay in theological anthropology on contemporary culture, and where one chapter, representing about a tenth of the whole text, is devoted to the topic of culture.

In this context it is assumed that the text will be easily available to the reader. Hence these pages offer a guide to the main issues. The key definition or description is as follows (No. 53 – in my own translation):

> It is one of the marks of the human person to reach true and authentic humanity only through culture, that is, by cultivating natural gifts and values. Whenever human life is involved, nature and culture are intimately connected.
>
> In its general sense the word 'culture' stands for everything by which human beings refine and develop their various capacities of mind and body. It includes efforts to control the cosmos by knowledge or by work, as well as ways of humanizing social life within the family or civic community through the progress of customs and institutions.

It is significant that it begins by relating culture to the nature of the human person and by claiming that only through culture does a person arrive at authentic humanity. Immediately two foundation stones of Catholic thinking on culture become clear: that culture is intimately linked with the dignity of the person and with the call of freedom to become more fully human. These are notes that will sound again and again in Catholic commentaries of later decades.

Having established this basic perspective on culture, the text goes on to a more detailed description of what culture means. What is notable here is that the Council openly recognizes a shift in the understanding of culture today and indeed it balances three levels of meaning – the older sense of culture as self-'cultivation', a more phenomenological or anthropological view of culture as embodied in a whole range of social systems and expressions, and thirdly, an explicit recognition of the plurality of cultures.

At first the conciliar statement lists five dimensions of human development, three of which (1, 4, 5) belong within the classical meaning of culture, while the remaining two (2, 3) come from a more sociological understanding of culture and indicate concrete ways in which human development embodies itself in social realities:

1. cultivating one's intellectual and physical gifts (this intra-personal sense of culture summarizes the more traditional meaning of the word);
2. mastery of the earth through research and through work (here the Council intends to include the modern spheres of science and technology);
3. efforts to humanize society and family life by means of traditions and institutions (this covers evolution in such areas as politics, education, health, and all the complex factors that create modern societies);
4. spiritual self-expression of the great human hopes (thus joining the world of art to the world of religious faith);
5. preserving and communicating inspiring visions of life for the 'progress' of humankind (this touches on culture as transmission of values from the past to the future).

Having mingled these characteristics of humanistic and empirical culture, the Council turns to another specifically modern interpretation. Stating explicitly that it is considering the 'historical and social' dimensions of culture, it adds that contemporary sociology and anthropology bring to light a 'plurality of cultures'. It then gives a list of reasons why different 'styles of living' and 'scales of value' exist: these are grounded in differences in work patterns, in religious world-views, in ways of self-expression, as well as in social structures or institutions. In short, the Council in a few short sentences moves from the traditional or 'high' view of culture as self-transcendence to two newer horizons: the sense of culture as involving living conditions, social organizations and assumptions, and an acknowledgment of the different forms of life that account for cultural diversity throughout history.

Thus, this paragraph 53 links the older meaning of culture – as a field of human growth and of intellectual or aesthetic achievement – with the more empirical sense of culture (or cultures) as embodied in social structures and in historically diverse approaches to life. This key section of *Gaudium et Spes* ends by noting that each human community, with its specific history and geography, has its own inheritance of wisdom and its own way of fostering basic human values; hence, even if not stated openly, it is evident that there can be no 'uncultured' nations and the monopoly exercised by the more aristocratic meaning of culture has been broken for good.

The remainder of the chapter on culture is neatly divided into three named sub-sections with three paragraphs within each section. The first section deals with the contemporary cultural context, the second with principles of cultural development, and the third with responsibilities of believers in the cultural field. For present purposes, it will be enough to touch on some of the main topics that arise, especially those that will continue to be central in Catholic reflection on culture in later decades. Each paragraph can be given a brief title, sometimes echoing the official headings in the text, followed by a short account of the key points.

A radically different context.   Paragraph 54 speaks of a 'new age of human history', where social changes have brought about a 'mass culture' that has enormous impact on how people think and act. Interestingly, this paragraph is couched in a deliberately descriptive tone, with no hint of negative judgement concerning mass culture; indeed, it expresses a hope that these new conditions can build a more 'universal' culture, expressing the 'unity' of humankind, and yet respecting the 'particular features' of local cultures.

Historical and cultural consciousness.   Paragraph 55, with a title speaking of humanity as 'author of culture', moves on to speak of 'a new humanism being born' in today's world. This involves a deeper awareness of 'autonomy and responsibility' felt by people today before the task of building up 'their community's culture'. Again this characteristic is seen in a very positive light as indicating 'spiritual and moral maturity' before the calls of history.

Honest facing of dangers.   As if admitting that the previous two paragraphs might be excessively optimistic, paragraph 56 lists some of the contradictions and ambiguities in contemporary culture, but it does so through a series of questions, thus avoiding any appearance of condemnation or criticism. These questions raise such issues as the danger of new cultural forms undermining traditional wisdom, how to reconcile specialization with a capacity for wonder, or how to prevent 'legitimate autonomy of culture' becoming narrowly secularist and anti-religious.

Cultural tasks in the light of faith.   Paragraph 57 is the first of three devoted to a more specifically theological understanding of the whole field of culture, and this first paragraph situates the calls of culture within the overall vocation of Christians. The final destiny of life with God should energize rather than diminish the engagement of believers in the humanization of this world. Hence cultural activities are central to the Christian calling. The text goes on to admit that the impact of science and technology can narrow one's sense of truth and produce a false self-sufficiency, but it immediately denies that such ills follow from contemporary culture itself. Once again there is a deliberate effort to evaluate modern culture as a bearer of 'positive values', which can prepare people for the gospel message and even be grounded in divine love.

Relationship between gospel and culture.   If the previous paragraph dealt with faith and culture, this shifts the focus to gospel and culture. In view of our subsequent chapter here on the work of the World Council of Churches, it is worth noting that even the order of presentation of these two sections seems significant. Faith-and-culture will remain a principal category for Catholic reflection in later decades and it raises issues of responding creatively to this particular moment of human history in the light of faith. Gospel-and-culture, however, will be the preferred expression at the heart of WCC explorations, and, as will be seen, it raises a rather different set of concerns about how gospel revelation can be expressed in different cultures. In broad terms (as will be seen later), Catholic underlying assumptions seem more anthropological and philosophical, whereas the WCC priorities seem more evangelical and socio-political.

Paragraph 58 begins by evoking the cultural nature of revelation itself, where God's progressive self-communication adapted itself to the culture of different ages. Against this background it unites two perspectives concerning evangelization (without using that word which entered Catholic discourse from the mid-seventies on): that the gospel message transcends all cultures, purifying and transforming them, and yet the mission of the Church is to embody the gospel in different cultures, enriching the culture and being herself enriched in the process. The revelation of God, not being a magic power but a word entrusted to humanity, needs constant communication in new situations and this naturally entails cultural sensitivity. This is a basis for what will later be called inculturation.

In addition this paragraph contains the important assertion that the Church has no fixed relationship with any culture: this is in the spirit of an eloquent speech of Cardinal Lercaro during the Council debate, when he argued that the Church should embrace a certain cultural poverty, not clinging to the riches of the past even in thought systems or artistic expressions; while always rooted in Scripture, the Church should explore the languages of contemporary culture and its emerging values. New credibility and religious force would be found from such humility, according to Lercaro.

Rightful autonomy of culture.   Paragraph 59 comments on conditions necessary to ensure the authentic development of culture. Culture flows from a person's rational and social nature and should defend the human person and serve the good of the community. Therefore it is called to foster wonder and awareness on different levels – religious, moral and social. But in order to safeguard these ideal goals of culture, its legitimate independence needs to be recognized – including liberty of research, expression and information. Above all, culture has the right not to be manipulated by those in power.

The remaining three paragraphs are more practical in focus and indeed some of the positions already seem dated or over-cautious in expression.

The right to culture.   Paragraph 60 speaks of making cultural bene-fits available to all. On the level of 'basic culture', there are problems such as illiteracy, or conditions of life or work that are dehumanizing. Ideally all should have the opportunity to develop themselves, and in this context the document refers to women sharing fully in cultural life. Underlying this paragraph is the assumption that cultural 'goods' are not just a luxury for the rich, but something essential to all human life. The implicit philosophy is that because self-development is a duty of each person's human freedom, access to cultural opportunities is a right.

The difficulty of cultural synthesis today.   Paragraph 61 recognizes that because of the complexity and specialization of different fields of culture, it is increasingly rare to be able to achieve an organic vision of life. Opportunities for education and for leisure have greatly expanded, but an 'integral culture' will not come about without a certain quality of reflective questioning, and some grasp of the crucial relevance of culture for the growth of the person.

The role of culture in Christian formation.   Paragraph 62 is the last and longest of the whole chapter on culture and bears the marks of being something of a dustbin for ideas that did not fit in easily in other parts of the text. Nevertheless it has a certain coherence and unity, which focuses on the issue of the relations between the Church and culture: it acknowledges tensions and shadows in different moments of history, but commits the Church to a constant dialogue with new forms of thought and art. This hope is grounded in the trust that truth cannot ultimately be contradictory and that fields of knowledge have their own autonomy. It is worth remarking that although many asked for explicit mention of the Galileo case in this context, it had been referred to in an earlier paragraph of *Gaudium et Spes* (36) and hence was not mentioned again here. However, the text does take account of a gap between artists and the Church in modern times; it calls for an acknowledgement of new forms of art and encourages their presence in places of worship.

Among other important themes mentioned here are the following: an openness to new vistas in contemporary thinking in order to be able to discern new developments in the light of faith; the need for inter-disciplinary work in theology; encouragement for lay people to study theology; the need for freedom of expression by experts in various fields.

Conclusion

Reading this chapter of Vatican II some thirty years later, a number of points call for comment. First, this text has proved prophetic: even if during the Council it was not one of the more dramatic developments, with the passing of time its significance has grown and indeed the theme of culture has become quite central in the thinking of Pope John Paul II. Secondly, these statements of the Council now seem almost innocently optimistic in their approach: this was due to a deliberate option on the part of the council to avoid condemnations and to give a sympathetic pastoral reading of the modern situation. Thirdly, many of the key issues treated in this chapter continue to be central in the decades ahead, and hence Church reflection concerning culture still looks back to *Gaudium et Spes* as its *magna charta*. This will become obvious in our next section dealing with post-conciliar Catholic developments in this field and in particular with the extraordinary prominence given to culture by Pope John Paul II.

Chapter Four

Catholic Developments since 1965

> American culture is desperate for a conversation about public issues
> set in a moral framework ... Encourage that conversation, build a
> sense of community that flows from your practice and your conviction
> that Catholics and ideas are not a contradiction in terms.
>
> (Margaret O'Brien Steinfels)[1]

> The central debate of our time has switched increasingly from politics
> and economics to culture. (Michael Novak)[2]

The changing role of culture in official Catholic approaches since
1965 can be told in two parts. One is like a brief prologue: it concerns
the 1974 Synod of Bishops on evangelization and the resulting text
of Pope Paul VI entitled *Evangelii nuntiandi* (1975) which deals in
part with 'evangelization of culture'. The second part will summarize the enormous amount of attention given to culture since John
Paul II was elected Pope in 1978, and will try to identify the principal
lines of reflection that have emerged during this period.

A more confrontative approach

It is sometimes claimed that *Evangelii nuntiandi* is the most
important of post-conciliar papal documents and the one that has
had the most lasting impact. Coming as it did exactly ten years after
the end of the Council, this 'apostolic exhortation' is couched in an
unusually energetic style for such an official text. From the outset it
voices an urgency about how the 'hidden energy of the Good News'
can find 'evangelical force capable of really transforming the people
of this century' (No. 4). It identifies evangelization as 'the essential
mission of the Church' (No. 14), and the source of her identity.
It also asserts that the Church remains always in need of being
'evangelized by constant conversion and renewal, in order to evan-

gelize the world with credibility' (No. 15). All this is the context within which Pope Paul arrives at the first major ecclesial statement concerning 'evangelization of culture'.

Just prior to paragraph 20 which is devoted entirely to this topic, evangelization itself is described as 'bringing the Good News into all the strata of humanity and through its influence transforming humanity from within' (No. 18). The next paragraph focuses on the implications of these different 'strata', insisting that it involves 'affecting and as it were upsetting, through the power of the gospel, mankind's criteria of judgement, determining values, points of interest, lines of thought, sources of inspiration and models of life, which are in contrast with the Word of God' (No. 19). Thus the evangelization in question will seek to change the cultural assumptions of people: the implication is that the dominant criteria of common sense are often in silent conflict with the gospel. If so, then evangelization has to include a new and ambitious goal – the Christian transformation of culture in its many senses.

The relevant section entitled 'evangelization of cultures' can be found in the 'anthology' chapter here. Its key points can be paraphrased as follows:

1. To transform cultures means going to the roots and not being content with surface appearances.

2. The gospel is independent of cultures but the Kingdom it proclaims has to be lived by people within their cultural realities; hence the gospel is not incompatible with any culture, in the sense of being able to enter a culture without becoming subject to that culture.

3. The 'drama of our time' lies in the gap that has opened up between culture and the gospel; healing this split is an essential dimension for evangelization today.

This tone of anxiety about the ambiguities of contemporary culture was not so present in the texts of Vatican II. Hence this landmark document of a decade later represents a shift in Catholic approaches to culture and one that will continue to have echoes in later years. Culture is taken as a convergence of many layers of significance – as acknowledged in Vatican II – but this complex phenomenon is now discerned religiously as being a potential blockage to the liberating

truth of the gospel. By invoking the metaphor of 'drama', this interpretation goes beyond Vatican II and recognizes an inevitable
conflict in the process of confronting cultures and of transforming
them with the vision of the gospel.

A new centrality for culture

The sheer quantity of explorations of culture in the speeches of Pope
John Paul II would merit a book in itself, and indeed at least one
such book exists in Spanish.[3] For present purposes, however, an
overview of key recurring themes will serve in order to identify the
principal issues that have emerged in these decades. Obviously
there are other sources that could be examined, including the work
of the Pontifical Council for Culture – founded by the Pope in 1982
– and which publishes a quarterly review entitled *Cultures and Faith*.
In addition there is a growing theological literature on cultural
topics within Catholic academic circles. However, the main source
for this discussion will be the discourses of Pope John Paul II. In
order to lighten the presentation, one long quotation of importance
will be found in the 'anthology' appendix; and to reduce the number
of notes, dates of the speeches will be given in parentheses in the
text.

The personality and the intellectual formation of Karol Wojtyla
provide the background for the exceptional emphasis which this
Pope has given to culture. With his previous experience in theatre
and poetry, his expertise in phenomological philosophy, his natural
tendency is anthropological – approaching even religious issues
with a keen sense of the drama of personal meaning and existential
choices. But to this humanistic vision, he also brings an acute sense
of the spiritual conflict of values at the heart of contemporary
history, and hence he views culture as a key zone for the saving of
humanity from reductive images of itself.

The American theologian Avery Dulles has written an article
entitled 'The Prophetic Humanism of John Paul II'. By this he means
that Pope Wojtyla (as the Italians often call him) thinks within a
certain set of converging concerns: a longing to remind human
beings of their potentials for self-transcending living, in the face of
various forms of dehumanization; a spiritual sense of God's truth

because only in harmony with revelation do we find authentic fulfilment; an awareness that each person only discovers his or her genuine humanity through love within community and social solidarity – the opposite of this is 'alienation', a term the Pope borrows from Marx. Dulles has a section on culture which begins as follows:

> Culture has been a major concern of John Paul II from his early days, when he developed his talents for music, poetry and drama. Between 1977 and 1980 he published several important papers on the philosophy of culture . . . The Pope's theory of culture is thoroughly humanistic . . . Everyone lives according to some culture, which determines the mode of one's existence. Culture, as a human achievement, involves our capacity for self-creation, which in turn radiates into the world of products. Culture is a materialization of the human spirit and at the same time a spiritualization of matter. It thus serves to render our world more human.[4]

This priority given to culture can be confirmed in more than one personal statement of the Pope himself. In November 1979, just over a year after his election, he spoke to a special gathering of cardinals, called to reflect with him on major religious issues: 'it will not have escaped your notice that personally I tend to have special interest for the problems of culture, of science and of art'. He went on to voice a claim he repeated on several later occasions: 'in this vital area the destiny of the Church and of the world are at stake in this closing stage of our century' (5.11.79).

In a similar personal vein the Pope said to a meeting of European intellectuals in December 1983: 'You are aware that the theme of culture as such, and even more so the relation between faith and culture, is one that I have pondered much, in the light of my different experiences as a scholar, a Christian, a priest, a bishop, and now as Pope' (16.12.83).

Three versions of culture

When analysing the account of culture offered by *Gaudium et Spes*, we saw that it brought together three main dimensions – humanist, empirical and local. This threefold distinction can serve both to divide and to unify the different ways in which the Pope treats culture. Thus in his many speeches on this theme, it is possible to distinguish three somewhat different meanings for the term 'culture', which we can label creative or humanizing culture, sociological or lived culture, and particular or local cultures. Although there is no watertight division between them, nevertheless they point to three significantly different fields of culture.

This can also be illustrated by the frequent practice of John Paul II during his visits to various countries. His programme will almost always include a meeting with 'people of culture', which means the artists, intellectuals, educators, and those involved in the world of mass media. This latter world he has described more than once as the primary Areopagus of our contemporary cultural world. His speech to such cultural leaders will often evoke the long history of relationship between religion and culture, contrasting this with the present situation, when many forms of culture remain closed within immanence and forgetful of transcendence. If culture is where human beings become more human, and if different cultures represent different ways of facing the question of the meaning of existence, then the whole future of humanity is intimately linked with whatever happens in the field of culture. In short, the Pope's typical call to the world of conscious or creative culture is to realize the high ideals that can guide it and can again shape human wisdom for today. 'Every culture is an effort to ponder the mystery of the world and in particular of the human person: it is a way of giving expression to the transcendent dimension of human life' (United Nations, 5.10.95).

A second use of the term 'culture' in papal discourses focuses rather on life-styles. If cultivating one's humanity is seen as essentially good (meaning 1) and if local traditions are to be respected for their spiritual depth (meaning 3), living passively within the pressures of modern society is viewed as deceptive and dangerous for basic human values. This meaning of 'culture' as lived assumptions can easily become an 'anti-culture'. The 'dominant culture' is a phrase usually used with negative connotations: 'so much of our dominant culture is a culture of flight from God' (USA, 6.10.95). Occasionally one finds different meanings coming together even in the same sentence: 'a culture that is not at the service of the individual is not a culture' (Peru, 15.5.88). In other words, culture remains an ambiguous human construct, needing constant discernment. The great humanist ideal can fall into self-contradiction, and authentic values of ideal culture are under threat in the actual culture of contemporary secularized societies.

In certain countries and continents the Pope may also have a meeting with representatives of indigenous or traditional cultures, and here his discourses have normally been both more concrete and more protective. The key message is that the locally inherited wisdom is a rich treasure to be preserved. It should cherish its own values – such as a sense of the sacred or a reverence for the family – and guard them against cultural oppression by more superficial cultural trends (the second sense here). This positive evaluation of minority traditions is occasionally qualified by acknowledgement of potentially ambiguous elements: a passage from the encyclical on missions mentions a danger 'of passing uncritically from a form of alienation from culture to an overestimation of culture. Since culture is a human creation [it] is therefore marked by sin' (*Redemptoris missio*, No. 54).

Foundations for a philosophy of culture

As far as creative or humanistic culture is concerned, the most far-reaching speech of the Pope was that delivered in Paris to the members of UNESCO in June 1980. A few crucial passages from this lengthy speech are given in the 'anthology' at the end of this book. In general it was an impassioned plea to keep the transcendence of the human being at the centre of any approach to culture, and hence not to identify culture only with cultural products or activities. Thus a person's subjective 'being' rather than more externalized 'having' is the source of culture, and the importance of culture is seen best in the light of an integral humanism (that last expression from Jacques Maritain was not used by the Pope but captures well the core of his argument).

With this basic vision, the Pope's presentation elaborated various principles for understanding culture:

1. Taking the human person in his or her 'integrality' means respecting the material and spiritual aspects of humanity; this non-abstract sense of the person in history is the basis for understanding culture.

2. Culture is the key zone where human beings grow into fullness of humanity.

3. The human being is both the subject or shaper of culture and also its object or goal.

4. Historically there has been an 'organic and constitutive link' between religion and culture.

5. Christianity in particular has been a creator of culture because of the value it places on the transcendence of the human person.

6. The primary task of culture is education, not in any narrow sense, but serving spirituality and moral culture.

7. A nation exists through and for its culture, which is sometimes the saviour of its very identity.

It is clear that this is a highly humanistic and philosophical perspective on culture, and such an approach is fundamental for John Paul II. Indeed this particular speech remains a cornerstone of his thinking and is often echoed or quoted by him in later years. Even though this UNESCO discourse builds on the treatment of culture in *Gaudium et Spes* (without ever citing it), it is much more ambitious in its intellectual range. When the Council spoke of humanity being the 'author of culture' (No. 55), it was referring to a new sense of responsibility for history in modern times. When John Paul II speaks of the human person being the subject or architect of culture, he is not thinking of a contemporary sensibility but of something in the very constitution of humanity. More penetratingly than Vatican II, he wants to ground the nature of culture in a reading of human nature as self-transcending. Frequently John Paul II offers variations on this metaphysical anthropology of culture, insisting that 'culture is of humanity, by humanity, and for humanity' (10.1.92).

Other key expressions of humanistic culture

With all this background it is clear that the Pope's natural bent is to ground his thinking on culture in a philosophy of the human person. Having paused on this UNESCO address, we can summarize later comments on this dimension of culture fairly schematically:

Culture as personal and communal.   John Paul II continually insists that culture is 'oriented to the realization of the person in all one's dimensions', but at the same time he stresses that culture belongs to a people: it is the 'particular way a people cultivates its relationship with nature, with others and with God' (15.5.82). In this sense, culture is never private but shared: it involves the 'common good of each people, the expression of its dignity, freedom and creativity' and a witness of its particular history (*Christifideles laici*, 1988, No. 44).

Quest for truth and love.   Different cultures throughout history represent different languages of exploring 'the question of the meaning of personal existence' (*Centesimus annus*, No. 24). But today's intellectual culture suffers from anthropological immanentism, separates ethics from truth, and suffers from widespread relativism (*Veritatis splendor*). The energy hidden in the depth of cultures is love, whereby they 'overcome their incurable finiteness' opening themselves to the mystery of God (22.5.82). Love is also the 'primordial need' of every culture (12.1.90).

Dangers of closedness.   Religion is an integral part of genuine culture but today's specialist culture runs the risk of becoming dehumanizing. Intellectual culture in particular can close in on itself and remain in 'silence about the transcendent dimension of humanity' or about 'the question of God' (1.11.82). The influence of secular world-views can damage the range and quality of human questioning which is at the heart of culture. 'A culture without universal values is not an authentic culture' (12.4.87).

Church concern for art and creativity.   Human self-transcendence expresses itself in privileged ways through 'creative genius' and especially where beauty becomes 'an expression of the absolute' (22.5.82). The very existence of the Pontifical Council for Culture (an initiative of John Paul II in 1982) symbolizes the commitment of the Church to the development of culture, and in particular that those involved in creative fields 'may feel that the Church recognizes them as persons devoted to the service of the true, the good and the beautiful' (13.1.89). The Church also counts on them to help people 'rediscover their memory' and 'revive their consciences' (10.1.92).

A privileged space for dialogue.   Although, as we shall see shortly, with the passage of time more attention has been given to pastoral discernment of the lived cultures of today, contact with intellectual and artistic culture remains a key area for dialogue, especially with non-believers. In this sense culture represents 'a fundamental dimension of the spirit, which places people in a relationship with one another and unites them in what is most truly theirs, namely, their common humanity' (25.3.93).

Culture as lived

A second and rather different dimension of culture has been increasingly the focus of the Pope's reflections. It is as if he started out in the early years of his papacy with a concentration on the self-conscious culture of artists and thinkers but gradually found himself giving more attention to the lived culture that is such a hidden power in today's world. The spur to deal with this second side of culture was primarily pastoral, as made explicit in a section of the Pope's letter founding the Pontifical Council for Culture in 1982. Having claimed for the second time in the same letter that human destiny is at stake in the field of culture, the text continues:

> Hence the importance for the Church, whose concern it is, of a careful and far-sighted pastoral activity with regard to culture, and in a particular way with regard to what is called living culture, that is, the whole of the principles and values which make up the ethos of a people: 'The synthesis between culture and faith is not just a demand of culture, but also of faith . . . A

faith which does not become culture is a faith which has not been fully received, not thoroughly thought through, not fully lived out.' (20.3.82).

(That final quotation is from a speech by the Pope of some months previously.) This passage is significant in various ways: for introducing the theme of pastoral discernment; for its challenging claim that faith should become culture (the basis for talking about creating a Christian culture, as will be seen); for its distinction between culture and living culture.

Discernment of new mentalities

It is notable that in his series of annual addresses to the Pontifical Council for Culture, John Paul II has increasingly focused on this pastoral call to understand the lived culture in terms of its humanizing or dehumanizing influences on people. He spoke of facing the 'new cultures' of the younger generations, of listening carefully to the 'latent hopes and aspirations' of people today, and of doing this with admiration and also 'a clear sense of discernment' (13.1.83). This task of interpreting the lived cultures has three characteristics: it seeks to understand local situations and emerging 'mentalities'; its purpose is to prepare and serve evangelization; and it would offer a critique of cultural oppression and the presence of an 'anti-culture' (16.1.84). In a period marked by 'profound changes in mentality', and when 'many cultural milieus remain still insensitive' to the gospel, the question becomes: 'how is the message of the Church accessible to the new cultures, to contemporary forms of understanding and of sensitivity?' (15.1.85).

Even these brief references are proof of a broadening of the agenda. The mission of the Pontifical Council for Culture was not simply a matter of contact with the intellectual and creative world but also of pastoral reflection on the changing sensibilities of people today. The term 'spiritual discernment' appears with increasing frequency – to indicate a spiritual sifting of traits of readiness and sources of closedness for faith. Also much repeated is the link between 'the inculturation of the gospel and the evangelization of cultures' (15.1.86). In this series of addresses the Pope often refers to inculturation, but never limits it to so-called mission territories; instead he extends it to all cultural contexts of today. It becomes a question of discovering the 'language' to reach people in their depths and this is described as 'a cultural and evangelical project of the first importance' (17.1.87). Moreover, such discerning reflection is part of a struggle between a 'cultural void' due to 'the pressures of a culture without spiritual roots' and the hope to 'humanize society and its institutions through the gospel' (10.1.92).

The possibility of a Christian culture

Although the expression has often been criticized (and is viewed with a certain suspicion within the World Council of Churches, as will be seen), John Paul II has not hesitated to speak of the need for a 'Christian culture'. He put this phrase into the title of the 1992 assembly of Latin American Bishops – 'New Evangelization, Human Development, Christian Culture'. To advocate that faith should become culture means simply that the gospel can and should permeate 'the ethos of a people, its essential attitudes, its institutions and all its structures'. To counter the absence of 'fundamental Christian values in the culture of modernity', evangelization today has to 'respond to this crisis of culture' and seek to generate 'a cultural alternative that is fully Christian' (12.10.92).

Thus to hope for a Christian culture need not imply a nostalgic regression to some medieval theocracy. Evangelization of culture means precisely that cultural life – in all its dimensions – can be inspired and transformed by the gospel. However, it must be admitted that the expression 'Christian culture' can give the impression of a return to an old-style uniformity. It needs balancing with a sense of the plurality of cultures, and indeed Fernando Miguens has argued that there can be 'no single Christian culture, but many possible versions of Christian culture; in other words, different cultures can be christianized, yet preserving their pluralism: one should not identify universalization with uniformity'.[5]

Conclusion

Even in this relatively brief summary, it is evident that culture occupies a position of prime importance for John Paul II. During a visit to the University of Riga in Latvia in 1993 he was asked unexpectedly to address a few words in Polish to a group of his co-nationals. He chose to speak – without a text – on culture and in the course of his improvised remarks offered a quasi-definition of culture as 'all that shapes the human person and the community in which one lives' (13.9.93). This is not the most elaborate or professional definition of culture but it is significant and revealing: it unites the Pope's typical personalism and his sense of community, and although this formulation does not exclude creative or conscious culture, it points more in the direction of lived culture.

As we have seen, Pope Wojtyla was by temperament and training more inclined to the 'higher' culture but his pastoral concern led him to pay attention to the vast field of sociological culture and especially to its trivializing impact. On a visit to the United States he revealed the positive and negative approaches together: 'Sometimes witnessing to Christ will mean drawing out of a culture the full meaning of its noblest intentions . . . At other times witnessing to Christ means challenging that culture, especially when the truth about the human person is under assault' (8.10.95). That tendency to raise critical questions about the dominant culture is one which is shared by the World Council of Churches, as will be seen in the course of the next chapter. It is also a key issue for any discerning spirituality of culture, which will be a principal theme in later chapters here.

Chapter Five

The World Council of Churches:
a Different Approach

Culture shapes the human voice that answers the voice of Christ.
(Bangkok Conference 1973)[1]

The gospel is not good news unless it engages the culture of its hearers in a way which takes seriously that culture's identity and integrity.
(Jerusalem Consultation 1995)[2]

As this book goes to press, the World Council of Churches is preparing for a major gathering on faith and culture to be held in Brazil. Organized by the section dealing with world mission and evangelism, the chosen title is 'Called to One Hope: the Gospel in Diverse Cultures'. This event represents the culmination of a long series of developments within the WCC, a story that has seen the issue of culture emerge from being either ignored or viewed mainly from a missionary perspective; now it is seen as a major theological concern with challenging implications for both the communication and the praxis of faith today.

This chapter offers a brief account of relevant developments within the WCC, mentioning some of the parallels to the Catholic Church's concerns, and also highlighting some significant differences of emphasis. Konrad Raiser, the General Secretary of the Council, has stressed that the current approach to culture is not simply a question of ideas (as in older discussion about Christianity and culture), nor is it primarily missiological. Instead the contemporary focus has returned to basic issues concerning the dynamic interaction between the Gospel and human cultures.

If the core of the gospel is the person of Jesus, Raiser holds that Christian truth is less propositional than an event unfolding in the relationship to God in Jesus Christ. Turning to the companion term 'culture', he insists that its principal meaning now comes from anthropology, thus breaking any easy identification of culture with civilization or with folklore. In Raiser's words,

> Culture is the expression of the identity of a human community. Culture refers to the delicate fabric of habits, symbols, artistic representations, tools, rules of behaviour, moral values and institutions through which the human community orders its relationships to nature, to other communities and to reality as a whole. Through processes of socialisation and through tradition, a culture is being transmitted to the following generations. In this sense, culture is specifically human; it is the second 'nature' of human beings in their social relationships. Any understanding of culture includes the language, history, family patterns, etc. of a given community.[3]

This substantial description of culture (reprinted with other texts in the 'anthology' chapter here) gathers together many strands in a way that is partly similar to and yet different from that adopted either by Vatican II or by UNESCO. Its highlighting of the 'identity' of 'community' is stronger than either of those other definitions. By contrast, Vatican II in 1965 (at least in its key paragraph 53) had approached culture largely in terms of a more person-centred humanism. Likewise the UNESCO account (1982) sought to offer a broad synthesis of the range of cultural activities without prioritizing. On the other hand this quasi-official WCC definition of 1994 does not mention spiritual or religious horizons explicitly or positively (unlike both Vatican II and UNESCO in this respect); instead it adds a comment that traditional cultures included 'religious symbolizations' while these have been separated from culture in modern societies.

Raiser's article goes on to discuss a tension between 'dialogical' and 'dialectical' understandings of the relationship between gospel and culture. The dialogue model builds on such gospel images as the leaven that penetrates the dough and insists that to be faithful to the Incarnation of Christ one has to embrace the human realities of culture rather than judge them from outside. But the dialectic model reminds Christians of the radical ambiguity of all cultures, of their potential to freeze into destructive and alienating forms, and hence the permanent need for prophetic resistance to any uncritical identification of culture with gospel.

Points of tension and of convergence

Raiser lists three thorny questions that ecumenical discussion encounters in this area.

1.   How can one protect the unique and unchanging gospel in the face of a diversity of *Christian* cultural forms? His solution lies in recognizing that there are no timeless expressions of the gospel: the one Christ now has many faces and all faith embodiments are cultural. Tension between the universal gospel and the local particularity is inevitable.

2.   If this is accepted, a fear of relativism arises: are there no criteria for evaluating true and false embodiments of faith? In his view the very question reveals a need for the gospel to become part of a local culture and yet maintain 'critical distance' in order to uncover life-denying aspects of a culture.

3.   Can we speak of a 'Christian culture'? Raiser tends to identify the very idea of a Christian culture with efforts to restore an impossible past in the more complex present.

Some comments by a previous secretary general, Emilio Castro, offer a crisp summary of insights on culture that have gradually became accepted in this period of WCC reflection.[4]

1.   Culture is not neutral: it can be an idolatrous influence and yet all cultures need to be encountered in a spirit of constructive dialogue.

2.   Cultures are human constructions, and as such bring a mixture of shadows and light. One can add that WCC uses the term 'discernment' less than in Catholic circles but advocates a similar combination of respect and evangelical judgement.

3.   Culture provides the 'scenario' or 'infrastructure' for the communication of the gospel but it is more than a passive frame of reference: unless evangelization is reduced to 'soul territory' and

forgets about Christian responsibility for the public realm and for all of creation, it includes a task of constant humanization.

The evolving synthesis within WCC reflection

In 1994 S. Wesley Ariarajah published an excellent pamphlet that summarizes the discussion on culture over recent decades. Entitled *Gospel and Culture*, it stresses that although the debates have been occasionally repetitive, there is now a significant consensus on the general importance of culture for theology and mission, and also on how to approach some of the key questions involved.[5]

Even before the foundation of the WCC in 1948, the topic of culture was present, if not always explicitly, in many of the deliberations of the series of world mission conferences that started with Edinburgh in 1910. Before the Second World War the tendency was to speak more about the encounter of the gospel with people's *religions*, and to assume that cultures were simply the outer expressions of different religious systems. 'Pagan' cultures were simply 'in error' and hence converts were expected to renounce both their former religion and culture and take on the 'Christian way of life'. If scant or merely negative attention was paid to culture, this neglect was also in tune with the dialectical theology dominant in those decades: Karl Barth and his followers stressed the discontinuity between the gospel and all human traditions, and they viewed even 'Christianity' with some suspicion – insofar as it can reduce itself to a 'religion' (or what today one might call an 'acculturated' religion).

The post-1945 situation, with all its woundedness, opened new horizons; the challenge of building up nations again brought a new focus on the local churches. Parallel to the process of decolonialization and the emergence of new nations, a different sense of selfhood was born in the younger churches of Asia and Africa. In the late forties there was much talk about the presentation of the gospel needing to 'adopt' values from people's cultures. Then in the fifties the word 'indigenization' became popular, meaning not only adaptation of worship but 'relating the gospel to local culture', in the words of the Kuala Lumpur assembly of 1959 (Ariarajah, p. 12). In 1963 the All Africa Conference of Churches came up with the statement that today can seem condescending but was then a courageous step (*ibid.*):

> Traditional African culture is not all bad; neither was everything good. As in all cultures, there were positive factors that held the culture together; there were negative factors which degraded human personality.

Thus a new stage of reflection opened up, which entailed overturning some of the previous theological assumptions within the missionary world. The New Delhi Assembly of the WCC of 1962 (its third general assembly but the first to be held outside the West) confirmed the more generous reading whereby the gospel is not simply disruptive of people's traditions, but can indeed be a force for saving what is deepest in a culture especially in an epoch of crisis and fragmentation. New Delhi suggested a relocation of the tensions involved in this field: instead of the Barthian approach of judgement of culture by the gospel, it diagnosed a more politico-cultural source of conflict in the 'unthinking imposition of Western customs' due in turn to the identification of 'Christian culture' with the West (Ariarajah, p. 25). This assembly, which took place during the same years that the Second Vatican Council was meeting, also attempted a short definition of culture as 'an integrated whole of ideas, traditions, institutions and customs, the setting of the life of a society, usually integrated around a religious faith' (*ibid.*).

The Bangkok 1973 missionary conference coined the statement (quoted at the head of this chapter) that 'culture shapes the human voice that answers the voice of Christ', but it also confronted the problem of how the universality of faith need not contradict its particularity. The Nairobi assembly of 1975 went further, viewing plurality as an opportunity for 'exchange between cultures'. In a tone that, as already mentioned, would not find exact parallels in official Catholic discourse, this assembly stated that the question of 'Christian culture' is 'loaded with cultural imperialism'. But it would find echo in Catholic thinking when it went on to affirm that 'no culture is closer to Jesus Christ than any other culture'. Since commitment to Christ 'takes different cultural forms', the community of the Church is 'called to relate itself to any culture critically, creatively, redemptively' (Ariarajah, p. 33).

Although S. Wesley Ariarajah holds that more recent WCC assemblies and world mission conferences have not gone further on the topic of culture, nevertheless these have been years of consolidating the consensus and of recognizing unresolved questions. He himself lists six areas of consensus, which can be paraphrased and expanded as follows (p. 34):

1. The gospel needs to root itself in each culture, finding expression in both life and worship.

2. The previous identification between Western culture and the gospel should be rejected openly, because, in the words of Vancouver (1983), the danger always remains of 'the gospel becoming captive to any culture'.

3. Sensitivity to cultures is crucial in all mission work; otherwise we fall back into attitudes of 'denigrating the receptor cultures' (Vancouver).

4. The gospel does not automatically accept everything in a culture, which is always a mixture of creativity and ambiguity: it also judges, challenges and transforms, and yet the gospel is also 'challenged by the cultures in which it finds itself' to create authentic expressions of Christian life (WCC Central Committee, Johannesburg, January 1994).

5. In an era of such cultural change, one needs to give special attention to the world impact of a secular and technological culture, and how the dominant culture can be intolerant of minority identity.

6. Another ecumenism is needed whereby Christians respect a plurality of cultural expressions of faith among themselves.

With the possible exception of the last point, these key points find practically identical parallels in official Catholic statements of recent years. Therefore there is a notable convergence of viewpoints, even though there has been little explicit reference to one another.

No 'pure' gospel – no abstract culture

What are the main areas of clarity and of continuing difficulty within the WCC understanding of gospel-and-culture? It has become clearer that theoretical convergences can sound empty unless they are tested in practice. In recent WCC commentaries a lurking idealism has been criticized, one that implies some 'pure gospel' that remains untainted by culture and therefore can be injected, as it were, into the messy field of culture. In theory the transcultural independence of the gospel is widely accepted, but in practice the gospel comes to us in cultural forms. This insight found concise formulation in a booklet of guidelines prepared for local groups: 'The gospel transcends every culture, but it is never accessible apart from its embodiment to specific cultures'.[6]

Especially because of a controversial presentation by a Korean speaker, Professor Chung Hyun-Kyung, at the Canberra assembly of 1991, the issue of 'syncretism' has become a major worry for some members of the WCC. Reluctant to accept her evocation of the Spirit of God in someone like Malcolm X or the suffering rain forests of the Amazon or in goddesses from native religions, Orthodox representatives (and more ordinary orthodox without the capital letter) found themselves wanting to define some 'limits of diversity'.

The fine essay by Ariarajah ends by expressing some doubts and disappointments. He notes that some WCC discussions of these issues have been going round in circles, 'taking both an affirmative and cautionary approach to culture' (p. 45). Exactly the same remark could be made of Vatican or Papal statements in these years, even though the assumptions would be different in various respects. As already mentioned, Catholic thinking in this area seems to draw on a more humanist or philosophical sense of culture, and refers to the long history of shared vision within 'Christian culture'. Besides, because of the higher emphasis on authority within Catholic practice, expressions of painful diversity at official level are much less frequent. On other issues, however, the evolution of Catholic discourse on culture in recent times shows many parallels to that of the WCC. There are some significant differences of vocabulary (the Catholic preference to stress 'discernment of culture', as part of 'evangelization of culture' and 'inculturation of the gospel') but on the whole many guiding insights concerning cultural issues are shared by both Catholics and the World Council of Churches.

Ariarajah traces a fundamental difficulty to the formulation 'gospel *and* culture': this can imply an unhelpful dualism, where the gospel appears 'culture-free' and where a culture is 'devoid of gospel values until in some sense transformed by it' (p. 45). In much the same spirit Christopher Duraisingh has argued that all this discussion concerning culture needs a different 'methodological approach', less deductive and less focused on a 'generic' or abstract notion of culture, and more inductive, grappling with the plurality of cultures. And he links this with the inescapable culturality of the gospel: 'while the gospel is never identical to nor is it exhausted by any particular expression of it, it is not available to us apart from its embodiments in specific cultures'.[7] As noted already, Catholic discussion usually speaks of 'faith and culture' rather than 'gospel', and hence avoids some of these pitfalls, faith having more clearly a human and cultural dimension.

Significance of the 1996 fourfold agenda

As a summary of current WCC concerns and searchings, one can take the four proposed sub-divisions of the 1996 meeting.

1. *'Authentic witness within each culture'* The key word is 'within' – a point echoed in Catholic discussions of inculturation. This is an important preposition, and one which is better than the problematic conjunction 'and' (of gospel *and* culture), or than the expression 'witness to culture' (as if culture were a passive object of evangelization). This heading stresses the particularity of each culture and the need for culturally sensitive witness to the gospel vision.

The WCC has produced some pamphlets to aid group reflection on these themes and under this first focus some excellent questions such as the following are proposed:[8]

• Where is the gospel comfortable in your culture? Where is it out of place? Do gospel values and cultural values lead you to different actions?

- How do different aspects of your culture enable you to understand the gospel in a fresh way?
- Do you see the gospel as something given to us, or as the recognition of God's activity in the world?
- Are there issues in your culture that call for change in order to be faithful to the gospel?
- In what ways have the understanding of the gospel and the practice of Christian life become captive to cultural norms?
- Can you identify life-affirming and life-denying aspects within your surrounding culture?

2. *'Gospel and identity in community'*   This will deal with the more 'structural dimensions' of culture and how power relationships can manipulate cultures. It will study, for instance, how a dominant and global 'mega-culture', with its powerful market and media pressures, can be a destructive and secularizing influence, and reflect on how the gospel can be a source of a liberating culture of resistance. Hence the agenda opens up the whole issue of secularism and the impact of consumerist life-styles as promoted by the culture of images and the mass media.

In addition this topic recognizes that authentic self-expression by minority or ethnic cultures may be crushed in the name of uniformity; alternatively, narrowly nationalistic claims for identity may be a source of division and even violence against the human community.

Among the discussion questions suggested for this second focus are the following:

- In what ways can Christians acknowledge complicity in the oppression of minority cultures?
- What cultural factors foster situations where the rights of women are denied or where the poor are excluded from full participation in the community?
- Where is there an uncritical alliance between religious/cultural vested interests and political power?
- What is the mission of the Church in contexts where communal conflicts on the basis of religion are perpetuated?

- In what ways are Christians called to be counter-cultural in the face of value systems contrary to the gospel?
- How can Christian congregations be prophetic before such transnational forces as the media and market economy?

3. *'Local congregations in pluralistic societies'* This section touches on inculturation and issues that are important in particular local contexts. It acknowledges the new complexity of culture caused sometimes by the presence of other religions in a given country or else by plural identities within individual Christian communities. If the previous heading touched on the vast international influences at work in today's world, this focus invites a complementary attention to concrete situations, encouraging a search for a genuinely indigenous faith language.

Again the booklet on 'study process' offers a useful set of questions for discussion, from which the following can be paraphrased:

- How much is the celebration of the liturgy expressed in local cultural idioms and capable of relating to the day-to-day life of the community?
- How would you go about a 'rereading' of the gospel in your context?
- How can the concrete situations of daily life find a place in spirituality?
- Are there ways of bringing 'youth culture' into more active interaction with the gospel?
- How inclusive is your congregation, in the sense of encouraging the participation of those on the margins of society? What can foster a relationship of dialogue with people of different cultures and religious traditions?

4. *'One gospel – diverse cultures'* This is where the thorny questions of syncretism and of limits to diversity have to be faced. More positively under this heading the hope is to celebrate some of the cross-cultural richness that is possible when the gospel is genuinely rooted (or as Catholic discourse would say, inculturated: the WCC has not made this term so central).

From a long list of questions for reflection, the following can be selected as indicative of the agenda:

- How can the witness of Christians who belong to another culture challenge, judge and enrich you?
- What are some 'signs of authenticity' whereby contextual expressions of the gospel can be assessed? Can there be universally applicable criteria?
- When does a way of evangelism become coercive and lead to proselytism?
- How can the churches function as agents of reconciliation across cultural divides?

It is obvious that these recent publications of the WCC represent a great step forward in the whole field of reflection on culture from the point of view of Christian faith. In some aspects they are remarkably similar to Catholic perceptions; in other ways they raise different issues and approach the whole field from a somewhat different angle. In their reading of the contemporary culture both Catholic and WCC commentators recognize certain key features of today's context: a realization of the omnipresence of culture – in its many levels – as a shaping but ambiguous influence on religious faith; the evolution of a global culture that can be the carrier of a secularist ideology; the struggle for particular cultural identities as both valid and yet capable of dangerous militancy today; a sharper awareness of cultural pluralism and of the challenge to incarnate Christian faith in ever new ways appropriate to local needs and sensibilities.

In short, there is an inescapable doubleness of culture as a source of possible deception and yet as a stimulus for new languages of faith. On the one hand people are seldom 'conscious of the cultural captivity of their understanding of the gospel'; on the other hand, we have not appreciated enough how cultures positively 'shape our response to Christ and open the gospel story for us in a fresh and wondrous variety of ways'.[9] That recognition of culture as both dangerous to faith and essential for faith is central to any theological reflection in this field: culture can indeed block the hearing of the Word but it is also the human zone of imagination most capable of fostering new languages of faith worthy of today's emerging sensibilities.

Chapter Six

Incoming Tides of Modernity

Modernity is the transitory, the fugitive, the contingent, the half of art whose other half is the eternal and the unchangeable.

(Charles Baudelaire, 1860)[1]

The parameters of our world-view are the presuppositions of a scientific culture. (Jane Collier)[2]

The transformations which ushered in modernity tore the individual from its stable moorings in traditions and structures. (Stuart Hall)[3]

The sentences just quoted are typical expressions of the crisis caused by the arrival of modernity, especially in Europe. Modernity stands for a cultural condition, as distinct from modernization which refers to more technical developments such as means of transport or of production. The two went hand in hand, as will be seen, but the end result was a greatly altered context for human belonging and human self-understanding, entailing a gradual but total break with pre-modern ways of life. It is a story that has been told many times and in many different tones. Sometimes it is narrated as a drama, hinging on a tension between scientific thinking and an increasingly lonely or homeless self. The arrival of modernity has often been linked to one or other event or historical moment; however it is better to think of it as a long incoming tide over centuries. One can identify particular 'waves' but, from the perspective of faith, modernity is a slowly accumulating phenomenon, resulting in a set of assumptions that made religious adherence of an older kind untenable for masses of people.

Since the long pastoral history of Christianity had been formed by pre-modern assumptions, suited to a village or largely rural society, the arrival of modernity posed a major cultural challenge for the Church. The embodiments and roots of faith that had proved

sturdy in a simpler culture inevitably became less fruitful and even
counter-productive in this emerging cultural situation. Hence it is
hardly surprising that Church responses remained negative for a
long time and that only with the Second Vatican Council did the
Catholic Church enter into a more open dialogue and opt for a more
positive interpretation of modernity. Some have commented that
this reconciliation is a classic example of the Church arriving on the
scene in time to embrace what was being severely questioned, just
before 'the modernity which the Council seemed to endorse has
been converted into postmodernity'.[4] Others have accused the
Council of bending over backwards to the extent of offering an
excessively rosy portrayal of modernity. The perspectives elaborated by the Council on culture were explored in Chapter 3. Religious
interpretations of modern culture will be the theme of Chapter 7.
The issue of postmodernity will then be dealt with in Chapter 8. The
aim here is to introduce the terms of the debate by offering a sketch
of the evolution of modernity and its significance.

Successive waves of modernity

With a certain irony Leszek Kolakowski has remarked that 'how far
back modernity may be extended depends, of course, on what
we believe constitutes the meaning of the notion'.[5] Indeed many
candidates have been presented as claiming to be *the* origin of
modernity. But clearly any competition of this kind that expects to
produce a sole victor is ill conceived. Modernity is best viewed as
a complex phenomenon, a product of converging forces through
various centuries.

The long debate about its possible beginnings serves, however, to
identify the many ingredients that make the accumulating reality
called modernity – at least as regards the Western world. According
to Louis Dupré, the origins of this phenomenon can be placed as
far back as the nominalist school of philosophy and subsequent
intellectual changes between 1400 and 1600. In his view that
separation of words from reality became a seedbed for later
fragmentations, and thus the complex story of modernity entails a
'spiritual revolution' over several centuries.[6] Once the emerging
modern individual feels no longer any embeddedness in the sur-

rounding world, religious anchors decay almost automatically. For Dupré the medieval divorce of the knower from the known opened the door for later claims that self-expression was *the* source of human meaning. This in turn became the cause of a gradual erosion of a religious sense of transcendence. If self is all, who needs society or religion or even culture? In this way alienation comes to be part of the lived assumptions of modernity.

Other commentators suggest more predictable moments from about 1500 on, showing how modernity gradually produced a new culture over about four hundred years. For instance, the Renaissance brought a whole new self-awareness of history, of humanism and of individuality, symbolized by the new dignity of the body in the art of Michelangelo, or by the new drama of individual consciousness in the plays of Shakespeare. Another strong candidate as seedbed of modernity overlaps in time with the Renaissance: the Protestant Reformation is credited by many scholars with being an essential stepping stone in the formation of 'modern' culture, especially through its stress on the relation between the individual conscience and God, independent of mediations such as religious institutions. And of course the spread of the Reformation was deeply linked to a technological breakthrough: it exploited to the full the opportunities provided by the new era of printing, the so-called Gutenberg Revolution.

From both the Renaissance and the Reformation a new sense of the individual entered Western culture. Some time later come the developments in philosophy associated with Descartes, significant for the parallel phenomena of rationalism and subjectivism. Intimately connected with this rationalism is the Scientific Revolution with its new stress on empirical criteria of truth, and the consequent clash with an unready older culture symbolized in the famous Galileo case.

The significance of this period of early modernity was captured with eloquence and authority by Hannah Arendt:

> Three great events stand at the threshold of the modern age and determine its character: the discovery of America and the ensuing exploration of the whole earth; the Reformation, which by expropriating ecclesiastical and monastic possessions

started the two-fold process of individual expropriation and
the accumulation of social wealth; the invention of the telescope
and the development of a new science that considers the nature
of the earth from the viewpoint of the universe.[7]

From these precise beginnings modernity went on, in her interpretation, to foster a new self-image of humanity – one rooted in the
'principle of utility'[8] and neglectful of larger horizons of personal
action and creative freedom.

Moving forward a century or so, many would see modernity as
rooted in the so-called Enlightenment with its insistence on the
right to freedom on various levels, freedom of thought, freedom of
speech, freedom from religious control, and so on. Inevitably linked
with this is the whole political movement most clearly embodied in
the American and French Revolutions, which inaugurated different
forms of democracy. Enlightenment and Revolution together represent a certain revolt against institutions and against older forms of
authority, and because of this both of these developments undoubtedly frightened the nineteenth-century Catholic Church, and caused
a response of suspicion and resistance.

Looking more to social rather than intellectual or political history,
one has to mention the Industrial Revolution, the arrival of capitalism as a dominant economic system, and the resulting upheaval
of urbanization. Modernization – as the institutionalizing of new
methods of production and related life-styles – is linked here with
modernity as a new cultural consciousness. England was probably
the first country in world history to have the majority of its popu-
lation living in towns and cities of more than about 10,000 people,
something that occurred around 1830 or so, largely due to the new
technology of the railway. Industrialization also represented a major
crisis for how we live together as human beings, since it brought
about a historically new phenomenon known as mass society; as
such it is often criticized for its erosion of older forms of community
and the introduction of a mass-produced commodity culture. At the
same time work-patterns changed and the new social situation had
an enormous impact on traditional rhythms of family life. Clearly,
all of these changes constituted a major challenge to traditional and
more rural embodiments of religious faith.

The aspects of modernity already mentioned are often interpreted as cultural sources of secularization, not only in the sense of a diminishing of the external control of the Church on social institutions, but also in the sense of a decline of religious adherence and the retreat of faith into the private realm. In this regard the nineteenth century also witnessed the birth of quasi-universal education and the consolidation of the new secular elites in the intellectual world. Universities became largely non-religious spheres of influence.

The twentieth century brought further developments that complete the complex accumulation that is modernity: electronic communications represent the biggest cultural revolution of recent times, with the arrival of radio, then television, and finally computers and information technology. The very rhythms of human consciousness have been altered by this world of fast-moving data and of images.

The significance of modernity

Even from this skeleton and necessarily simplistic history, some of the multiple strands of modernity come into view, as well as their impact on self-understanding. It altered the cultural conditions of possibility of the 'hearing' from which Christian faith is born: not only did the supportive and cohesive society of premodern times fade away, but during these centuries Churches found themselves fighting various rearguard actions on several fronts and facing new challenges to the credibility of faith itself.

According to Louis Dupré 'modernity is an *event* that has transformed the relation between the cosmos, its transcendent source, and its human interpreter'.[9] This implies that a living synthesis fell apart, and that deep connections between nature, God and human beings underwent drastic change. As early as 1610 the poet John Donne was expressing this sense of crisis in his 'First Anniversary':

> And new philosophy calls all in doubt
> The Element of fire is quite put out . . .
> 'Tis all in pieces, all coherence gone.

But if modernity, for some interpreters, meant loss, for others it meant gain, and in particular the emergence of human self-confidence in a way that was never so conscious in previous cultures. With the arrival of 'modern' culture human beings came to see themselves as capable of experiencing, understanding and being responsible for the world in excitingly new ways.

Three social thinkers: Habermas, Touraine, Taylor

There are whole libraries of philosophical and sociological interpretation of modernity. Here the aim is more modest – to identify some of its principal strands and how they impinge on religious faith. Consulting three of the specialists in the field will help to clarify the main issues.

Jürgen Habermas is famous for his defence of modernity in spite of what he acknowledges as its contradictions and dark sides. He finds it ironical that, with modernity, human beings became capable of shaping their own history and yet its very complexity deprived them of control over it. However, instead of joining those who view modernity as a failure and proclaim the new era of postmodernity, Habermas views it as a historical project that remains incomplete and that is worth continuing. In positive terms modernity 'is essentially characterized by the notion of individual freedom' in science, in self-determination and in self-realization. He sees these ideas as already part of our assumptions about life: 'they are inserted into everyday communicative practice, and thereby into the life-world'.[10] Certainly modernity was characterized by the dominance of rational-purposive methods of action, but its crucial contribution lies in the field of human autonomy; for Habermas these two realms need a third area of active communication in order to bridge the gap between reason and human values.

In a forceful and recent book Alain Touraine echoes this line of thinking from a different angle; he highlights 'the central cultural issue of the Subject', meaning the free individual who resists the imposed system as a matter of 'cultural choice' and thus becomes a social 'actor'.[11] Touraine's thesis rejects any easy identification of modernity with the forces of rationality alone, insisting that the divorce of reason from the realm of individual freedom underlies the disillusionment over modernity voiced for some generations now. It is as if one twin became dominant and the other retreated into a passive and private realm. Thus we have suffered a painful history of separation between the objective worlds of the economic system, work and technology and the subjective worlds of culture, meaning, freedom and creativity. In Touraine's view the contemporary dominance of the mass media only deepens this split because it is rooted in a liberal and consumerist ideology and because it seeks to dissolve the Subject's real freedom through the 'rule of commodities' and a 'rejection of transcendence' or the spiritual dimension of life.[12] Until we have some reconciling dialogue between rationality and subjectivity, we are condemned to a double dictatorship – of alienating systems and of narcissistic explorations of consciousness by an ultimately impotent self.

Rather like Habermas' insistence on communicative action, Touraine adds 'community' as a key area along with freedom and rationalization, and sees this trio as capable of rescuing us from the distortions of a modernity over-identified with reason and system and forgetful that we are 'creatures of desire and memory who belong to a culture'.[13] In this way he proposes to reunify the fragmented field of modernity and to overcome the 'limited' modernity we have so far experienced. Equally he hopes that a rediscovered role for cultural 'actors' can build up a resistance to the 'programmed' society of consumerism and self-interest. Although he is not offering an explicitly religious response to modern culture, he expresses in almost biblical language his urgent hope that the subject-as-actor assume ethical responsibility for the wounded of the world: 'Anyone who claims to be a Subject and ignores his neighbours who are being reduced to silence or death, is deceiving neither himself nor anyone else'.[14]

Touraine, however, is not naive about the conflictual nature of his thesis, and somewhat akin to Samuel Huntington (as mentioned in the Introduction here), he foresees 'conflict between cultures' as more radical now than in the classical era of industrial modernity, especially because of the lack of any community of vision today. But he adds, significantly, that 'cultural traditions are more alive than many people thought'.[15]

The Canadian philosopher Charles Taylor has offered some stimulating and positive readings of modernity. Like Touraine he focuses on the centrality of the self, but he views it more in terms of a whole shift in sensibility over centuries and he is also more interested in religious questions. Touraine and Dupré would also agree with him that many influences in modern culture push us towards a dangerous 'subject-centredness' and that 'overcoming it is a major task, both moral and aesthetic, of our time'.[16] Like other commentators on modernity Taylor discusses the role of disengaged reason and of the self-determining person; but in order to explain the new secularized consciousness, he gives special attention to two other factors: how ordinary family life changed its values with the rise of middle-class culture in the eighteenth century and the different kinds of inwardness and expressiveness that also came to be major values. Since, during the same period God was often presented as a distant explanation of the natural order, existence came to seem liveable without religious faith. In this way, and for the first time in history, one could cultivate a moral sensibility of benevolence and not necessarily believe in God.

Taylor traces how the self-expression central for Romanticism has narrowed today into the 'human potential movement' and into the 'shallowness' of a culture of subjectivist fulfilment. In this respect the final page of his major work affirms, with disarming simplicity, that 'we tend in our culture to stifle the spirit'.[17] It would be what he calls a 'mutilation' not to retrieve the spiritual aspirations that the complex evolution of the modern self neglected. Where Touraine puts his trust in a renewal of social agency to resist the inherited damage of modernity, Taylor looks more hopefully at the forgotten religious dimension of culture.

In a series of radio talks, this Canadian thinker develops his own discernment of the culture of modernity. He has misgivings about how self-absorbed individuals have lost a sense of any wider participation, or how technology seems to 'flatten' our lives, or how a 'soft' despotism of the state induces powerlessness in its citizens. He also worries about a serious 'loss of freedom' as the shadow side of modernity's great achievements.[18] But he remains a strong defender of those achievements and of the continuing potential of modernity to be redeemed in spite of everything. There is a major struggle going on between the more genuine and the more trivial faces of freedom, and hence the key question becomes how to sift out the wheat from the weeds, and how to nourish the wheat of authentic living today.

In Taylor's judgement, there is 'an extraordinary inarticulacy' about the 'constitutive ideals of modern culture', and this silence stems from a 'liberalism of neutrality'.[19] The alternative to this is not an easy and negative judgementalism about 'permissiveness'; rather one needs to inquire into the 'moral force behind notions like self-fulfilment', in order to save what is generous and valid at the heart of modernity.[20] In this respect he proposes two criteria for discernment:

> I want to show that modes that opt for self-fulfilment without regard (a) to the demands of our ties with others or (b) to demands of any kind emanating from something more or other than human desires or aspirations are self-defeating, that they destroy the conditions for realizing authenticity itself.[21]

In other words cut-off versions of individual freedom, that have little or no social conscience or little or no consciousness of ultimate values, will thereby lack authenticity. It is a quietly powerful argument for renewing the role of the social agent (like Touraine) and renewing the link to religious transcendence (like Dupré). It is also an impressive critique of the 'anthropocentrism' of modernity that can idolize 'choice itself', without reference to further meanings and goals.[22]

The challenge, as Taylor sees it, is to imagine self-responsible forms of life and in this way to rescue the fundamental achievement of modernity. The only way to fight fragmentation, he argues, is to 'strengthen identification with the political community', and towards this end our positive freedoms 'are not zero': 'we are free when we can remake the conditions of our own existence, when we can dominate the things that dominate us.'[23]

In a later section dealing with discernment of culture, more explicitly religious perspectives will be offered for responding to our cultural situation. However it is worth noting that from three such academic thinkers certain principal issues come to the fore that will also prove relevant for our later discussion: the sense of fragmentation, the divorce between social system and personal dimensions, the danger of closed-in individualism, the need for cultural analysis and for an honest facing of conflict areas, the threat of passivity represented by the media world of images, and most significant of all, the importance of community for any healing of the cultural ills of today.

Chapter Seven

Religious Responses to Modernity

The person who is able to see but unable to hear is much more troubled than the person who is able to hear but unable to see. Here is something characteristic of the big city. (Walter Benjamin)[1]

It would be profoundly ironic if, after all the beatings it has received from modernity, religion could somehow unintentionally help modernity save itself. (José Casanova)[2]

As seen in an earlier chapter, for the Catholic Church the Second Vatican Council represented a moment of conversion from attitudes of rigidity and suspicion before modernity to a remarkably more optimistic reading of contemporary culture. Indeed some of the statements of *Gaudium et Spes* would have been regarded as less than orthodox exactly a century previously, when official Church stances seemed to condemn practically all significant developments in thinking and politics. The Syllabus of Errors of 1864 became famous in this respect, with its refusal to reconcile itself 'with progress, with liberalism and with recent civilization'; while such a statement was understandable within the Italian situation of that time, it came to symbolize an extreme of ghetto reaction by the Church against the then modern world. As against this, one can set a 1994 statement of Pope John Paul II which offers a surprisingly positive evaluation of modernity: 'if by modernity we mean a convergence of conditions that permit a human being to express better his or her own maturity, spiritual, moral and cultural, in dialogue with the Creator and with creation, then the Church of the Council saw itself as the "soul" of modernity'.[3] What is implied here is an embracing of history as an adventure of freedom and a fresh interpretation of modernity as potential ground for Christian growth and authenticity, not simply as a negative challenge or danger to be warned against and avoided. Indeed this way of seeing modernity seems in harmony with that of the sociologist José Casanova cited in the epigraph to this chapter. Casanova studied the response of Catholicism to modernity in countries as different as Poland, Brazil, Spain and the United States, and came to the conclusion that where religion tries to resist the whole 'process of modern differentiation' and in particular the new sense of human autonomy born from the Enlightenment, it will simply fail and suffer 'religious decline'. But when religion discerns and accepts what is genuine within modernity, then not only can it find new authority for itself within the open societies of today, but it can save modernity from some of the 'inhuman logic' of its own unbalanced ideology.[4]

Apart from official Church positions, religious responses to modernity in recent decades fall predictably into two main families. Some commentators stress the breakdown of meaning and values, and advocate resistance to the damaging impact of modernity; this interpretation may or may not include a certain nostalgia for a previous unity of culture, but frequently it reads the cultural context as decidedly unfriendly to faith. On the other hand one finds an emphasis on the vast improvement of the human lot brought about by both the new ideas and the new technologies, and also a more positive reading of modern cultural horizons from the point of view of religion and faith.

Perhaps three major principles have guided theological reflection on culture within Catholicism during recent decades. First, culture is seen as a place of human transcendence and hence of creative encounter with God. Secondly, since all culture is a human construct, it remains a source of ambiguity always in need of discernment and purification. Thirdly, the culture of any particular place or time must play an essential role in the mediation of faith for people in diverse contexts of receptivity for the gospel.[5] Such general lines of approach are clearly of relevance to the whole inculturation debate, but they also underlie the long attempt to forge a religious interpretation of modernity.

Different generations of Catholic interpretation

Christopher Dawson was probably the most distinguished historian of culture working in the period prior to the Second Vatican Council. His constant emphasis was that in all the great civilizations, cultural creativity went hand in hand with religion. Looking at the whole trend of modernity he wondered if one can genuinely speak of a 'culture' if the religious horizon becomes so absent or impotent: if 'detached from spiritual aims and moral values', the living whole that is culture finds itself 'faced with a spiritual conflict of the most acute kind'.[6] As he pondered the 'weakness of Western culture' today, he saw modern education as having 'no sense of revelation'; in a society swamped with 'mass-mindedness', the older symbolic richness associated with cathedrals and worship seemed set aside. Therefore modernity (although Dawson does not use that word) had left people bereft of a 'spiritual sense of religion as an objective reality far transcending one's private experience'.[7] Modernity, in this light, is a case of unbalanced growth, where the mentalities of secularism and technology are incapable of healing the broken unity of a previously spiritual culture.

Among the classics of theological reflection on modernity, pride of place must be given to Romano Guardini's *The End of the Modern World*. Although dating from the late forties, it now seems a forerunner of many commentaries on postmodernity that have appeared within the last decade, and which express themselves with less elegance and much more jargon. In terms similar to those used by Touraine and Taylor forty years later, Guardini diagnosed a loss of an 'objective sense of belonging to existence' at the outset of the 'modern' period, and hence he saw a mixture of existential insecurity and 'the experience of subjectivity' as characterizing the new culture.[8] Modernity produced a phenomenon previously unknown to history, the autonomous personality without roots, and this in turn gave rise to a quest for 'culture' – in the sense of creating a human-based world of meanings. The secular values of early modernity often asserted themselves with hostility towards Christianity, so much so that faith went on the defensive and risked being perceived as merely negative in the eyes of history:

The defenders of Christianity complicated the problem by committing many a blunder in their battle with the new order, blunders which made Christianity seem an enemy of the human spirit.[9]

In Guardini's interpretation, such Christian critiques were largely impotent and ironically the real undermining of modernity came from within itself. The 'optimism about culture' at the roots of modernity was amply disproved by the tragedies of twentieth-century history. Its 'deliberate destructiveness' shocked people into a new distrust born from seeing through 'the illusions of the modern mind'.[10] Twenty years earlier, in one of his most eloquent texts, *Letters from Lake Como* (composed between 1923 and 1925), Guardini had pondered the death of an older organic culture, due to the rise of the technological and 'mass culture of our day'. In his darker moments he sensed that 'the battle for living culture has been lost', but then with more optimism he began to insist that 'our age is not just an external path that we tread; it is ourselves'.[11] Culture, in his view, can find renewed hope only through the retrieval of 'root virtues of earnestness and gravity, both grounded in truth', 'courage opposed to the looming chaos', and the spiritual art of asceticism to help distinguish 'right from wrong and ends from means'.[12]

Guardini is an excellent example of a Catholic response to the culture of modernity in terms of the scholarship of an older generation – the period prior to the Second Vatican Council. Unlike the Council he remains reluctant to recognize a wider anthropological meaning for 'culture', and hence he is slow to use that term for anything that does not serve the spiritual unity of society. He is deeply dismayed by the arrival of 'mass culture', interpreting it as inevitably impoverishing. And yet he obviously resists his own pessimism, and deliberately nourishes his hope in human creativity and the capacity to rediscover ways of wisdom in spite of, or possibly because of, the collapse of traditional culture.

In more recent years modernity has been viewed in terms rather of challenge than as a disaster area for religious faith. Hervé Carrier – who was the Secretary of the newly founded Pontifical Council for Culture for its first decade – has listed several sociological characteristics of modernity as constituting a new field for evangelization. He singles out the 'individualization of persons' as of particular relevance: as distinct from the premodern situation where roles in society were largely assigned to people by their family or situation, modernity fosters a desire for self-autonomy and sets a higher value than ever before on education and personal rights. These positive developments, however, can degenerate into narrow individualism, causing a tragic 'undermining of human communities' and also a crisis in family life.[13] In spite of the obvious fruits of technological progress, in making possible a different quality of existence, commentators have noted the contradictions that arise from modernity. In Carrier's words,

> By giving pride of place to efficiency and maximized productivity, the technical society has fostered a schizophrenic tendency in behaviour. Individuals are forced to play segmented and frustrating roles ... Rationality has supplanted reason, the understanding of overall objectives, and the value of personalized reflection. 'Leave your personal life aside' seems to be the message of modern business, government offices, supermarkets, unions, and political parties ... By a strange paradox, the affluent society has brought about a new form of alienation.[14]

If the shaping influences on people's receptivity for faith are so different from those of premodern times, then a certain 'cultural action' by believers becomes imperative: it is not enough to analyse the dominant life-styles or to describe the problem areas; the future depends on a discernment that can actually 'mould cultural reality'.[15]

Gospel and culture reflections in England

That call for faith to become culture has been paralleled in a whole movement of Christian reflection in Britain in recent years. Bishop Lesslie Newbigin returned to England after nearly forty years as a missionary with the Church of South India, only to find himself viewing the culture of his upbringing with more critical eyes. That contrast of experiences led him to reflect on the impact of post-Enlightenment Western culture on the rest of the world, as well as on its secularizing tendencies within Europe itself. He criticizes the presumption of 'an atomic individualism' and the privatized version of Christianity that dominated various forms of Protestantism. He also describes how missionaries brought dubious Western assumptions to traditional societies. Because of their excessive emphasis on individual conversion, many missionaries were insensitive to the community values already present in non-Western societies and were also unaware of the need to convert cultures and not just individuals.[16]

In different studies Newbigin traces the emergence of current Western cultural assumptions, and how, without it being clearly recognized at the time, they gradually made Christian faith socially marginal, if not actually incredible. While appreciating the great breakthroughs in scientific method since the seventeenth century, he discerns some negative side effects over how we think of truth and of purpose. The very success of empirical methods of experiment leads to the illusion that this is the only dependable form of truth. Where this assumption is accepted without qualification, the biblical picture of God finds itself in deep trouble. The disappearance of the concept of 'purpose' from science in the early modern period (the generations from Galileo to Newton, more or less) created ripples of influence well beyond the sphere of science. Until the arrival of modernity science had always presumed that it was uncovering, in some sense, the meaning of a God-given universe. 'Medieval thought saw divine purpose manifest everywhere in the world of nature', but the effect of the new science was to replace this explanatory approach with another – a world 'governed not by purpose but by natural laws of cause and effect'.[17]

Without being hostile to science, and noting in fact that more recent developments in physics and cosmology break entirely with the Newtonian model, Newbigin concludes that one cannot have dialogue between the gospel and modern culture without recognizing definite areas of contradiction. 'It is obvious that our modern Western world constitutes a plausibility structure within which the biblical account of things is simply unacceptable.'[18] Christian faith makes claims about truth and purpose that cannot be reduced to the psychological or the cultural or to private opinion – the only spheres where modernity is content to allow them to have sway. Without other criteria of truth, central Christian realities such as the resurrection of Jesus appear simply irrational in the light of these dominant ways of thinking.

This approach to questions of gospel and culture, initiated by Lesslie Newbigin and developed by others, unites two principal horizons: how intellectual and social history has created a radically different situation for religious belief and a missiological emphasis on the need for conversion of culture. In the intellectual sphere this analysis stresses the influence of an empiricist philosophy on the plausibility of faith, and in this light it sees modernity as causing a crisis over the credibility of religion. In addition, the lived culture is so greatly impressed by the intellectual respectability of science that it tends to accept unquestioningly the retreat of religious truth to areas of personal taste or autonomous choice. In terms of missiology, Newbigin himself has criticized an apparent hesitation over proclamation of the gospel within the World Council of Churches. If dialogue means simply a 'sharing of life' and if the 'richness of diversity' becomes a dominant value, what happens to the duty to announce the gospel as truth? In all this he discerns a danger that the Enlightenment version of modernity can tempt even committed Christians into a loss of self-confidence and an 'indifference to truth'.[19] As against this suspected failure of zeal, the call is to give faith a voice in the public world of culture and at the same time to encourage an intelligent analysis of the cultural blockages to Christian truth. One of the principal blockages is precisely the assumption that faith is so individual a matter as not to need any cultural embodiments. If that bias remains unchallenged, the very possibility of believing today can be undermined by the secularity of the culture. Similarly if Christian faith does not become culturally vocal and creative, it may become simply a zone of spiritual comfort for the separate self.

This line of interpretation has given rise to a programme or movement entitled 'Gospel and Culture',[20] whose tendency is to offer a fairly trenchant critique of the Enlightenment tradition in the light of Christian faith. Among characteristic judgements of this approach one can list the following:

- 'the privatization and relativization of religion which has taken place in Western culture over the past three centuries amounts to nothing less than a radical falsification of that [Christian] message'.[21]

- 'there is the dramatic phenomenon of the displacement of religion from the very centre of public life to the private sphere ... If the gospel is public truth, then it addresses not merely isolated individuals but persons-in-community'.[22]

- 'The reception of the Christian faith within a country is bound up with the "root paradigms" of that country's culture. If the underlying assumptions are not "Gospel-friendly", the Gospel in that country will not prosper ... It follows that a mission to our culture is needed quite as much as a mission to the individuals who live within that culture.'[23]

More theological responses to modernity

David Schindler, a Catholic theologian and editor of the quarterly *Communio*, would probably agree with those evaluations of the ills of modernity; however he seeks to offer a specifically theological analysis and to concentrate more on North American culture. According to his argument, the underlying ethos of American life links two aspects of modernity: the 'driving impulse to order the world without God' and a machine-like model of human relationships, where the person is viewed mainly in terms of control and efficiency.[24] Christians often lament the negative characteristics of culture today, as shown in consumerism, permissiveness, the abuse of power or the manipulation of human life itself; for Schindler such moralizing is insufficient. Instead, it becomes crucial to identify 'the deeper logic of self-centricity and externality' that rules people's culturally received visions of reality, and then to identify the fundamental clash between such a liberal and 'mechanistic culture' and the radically different vision of human relationships in the light of Christian faith.[25]

According to this analysis, the prevailing culture in North America fosters a utilitarian sense of the autonomy of the self, which manifests itself in 'arbitrary freedom' and in 'use' and 'domination' of others: 'there is a direct link between a subjectivity (or will) become arbitrary and an objectivity (or reason) become *techne*'.[26]

Schindler notes that America's religious heritage usually pictures God in strictly 'monotheistic' and 'masculine' fashion, just as the whole culture tends to see human beings as primarily active and productive.[27] Hence an uncontemplative theology has colluded with an externalist culture and a lop-sided sense of human autonomy. The radical answer has to lie in a different spirituality – more Christological, more Trinitarian, more Marian – because only in this way, according to Schindler, can the culture rediscover the religious sense whereby life is primarily received from God as gift. The opposing 'logic' at the root of modernity – and of its product, 'liberal democracy' – is one of secularization. Its principal flaw, from a Christian point of view, lies in the promotion of an isolated self-identity divorced from relationships. The response to this wounded-ness, Schindler insists, is not to reject 'the achievements of modernity' but rather to question them and to integrate them into a more relational philosophy.[28]

In line with Touraine and Taylor, Schindler sees hope in the possi-bility of deepening 'the interiority-subjectivity that had been the distinctive achievement of modernity'.[29] In other words, the subjec-tive wing of modernity, with its innovative sense of selfhood, remains not only redeemable but a vital entry point for Christian faith into today's culture. These commentators also highlight the whole zone of social belonging and responsibility as capable of healing the fragmenting forces of modernity. Like Newbegin who spoke of the need to convert culture, Schindler identifies the crucial area of transformation: 'a nature not formed in love will tend (of its inner "logic") to express itself in the mechanistic-instrumental patterns of thought and action'.[30] In spite of all its positive develop-ments, the overall impact of modernity is viewed as anti-Christian in its limiting of our self-images to the realms of the useful and the measurable.

These more sober evaluations of modernity represent a certain school of theology today, but there are other voices. Indeed theo-logians in this respect are described as falling into two opposing schools. There are those, such as Rahner, Schillebeeckx and Lonergan, who try to continue an Aquinas line of 'correlation' or positive learning from the culture. And there are those, such as de Lubac, von Balthasar and Ratzinger, more influenced by Bonaventure or earlier patristic writings, who stress the differentness of faith from any culture.[31] As will be seen in the chapter on inculturation, this can also be interpreted as a necessary tension between an incarnational and a redemptive focus in theology.

What is significant is that the pendulum has swung in recent years towards more caution about the encounter between faith and modernity – as exemplified in the Catholic and Protestant thinkers mentioned in these paragraphs. They see the fall-out from the European Enlightenment as responsible for many of the cultural pressures that weaken Christian faith: mechanistic thinking, a self-interested market economy that constricts human aspiration to consumerist needs, overweening scientism, reductive theories of human reason, relativism in education, a retreat of values to the private realm of individual fulfilment, and a portrayal of religion itself as a field of merely subjective choice. At the same time as secular thinkers were unmasking the illusions of modernity, Christian commentators, from their own perspective, were also identifying some of its shadows.

If this tendency to judge modernity severely seems to contrast with the more serene dialogue initiated by the Second Vatican Council, it is partly a question of different decades. Where the sixties sought to concentrate on the permanent human achievements of the modern age – especially in the field of freedom and of human dignity – the eighties were more inclined to stress the damage produced by the same complex phenomenon of modernity. The sixties needed to heal the long-standing and mutual incomprehension between Christianity and modernity, but the eighties, without going back on this recognition of positive developments, became more acutely aware that permanent and dehumanizing flaws remained within 'modern' culture. This new Christian critique of the roots of modernity will be of relevance when we come – later in this book – to questions of discerning the spiritual contexts of today and the lived culture that structures daily consciousness. Even if the debate has moved on from modernity to more complex issues of postmodernity, the principle challenges arising from modernity remain with us. Hence the varying responses listed in this chapter retain their interest and their validity.

Chapter Eight

The Postmodern Situation – Friend or Foe?

Exaggerated faith in 'science', along with a very confused idea of what science is, distorts a wide area of Western thought. (Mary Midgley)[1]

Postmodernity can be seen . . . as a re-enchantment *of the world that modernity tried hard to* dis-enchant. (Zygmunt Bauman)[2]

What are we to make of 'postmodernity'? From the outset, it is important to stress that it is not the same as 'postmodernism'. Even though not all users of these terms give them the same meaning, there is a tendency to use 'postmodernism' for the more *intellectual* school of thinking associated with Lyotard or Derrida, or even tracing its origins as far back as Nietzsche, and then to reserve 'postmodernity' for a wider *cultural* context that includes ways of life as well as forms of thinking, and which can be viewed more as a 'sensibility', or as 'postmodernity of the street'. The two realities are not completely separable. Both share a certain questioning of the achievements of modernity but whereas postmodern*ism* seems to remain largely in a mode of refutation, cultural postmodern*ity*, as will be seen, goes beyond negative critique and, in some instances, represents a search for liveable languages beyond the narrowness of modernity.

It is not surprising, therefore, to find conflicting religious interpretations of this phenomenon. For some believers it represents a new epistemological humility that opens doors to faith. For others it is a lethal form of relativism that undermines all truth claims. Perhaps both judgements are valid; they simply refer to very different aspects of the postmodern.

Although some initial space here needs to be given to 'postmodernism', the main focus will fall on 'postmodernity'. Since the main postmodernist tendencies are more vehemently negative than positive, one can summarize them as a set of ten commandments, commenting on how they overturn the typical positions of 'modern' thought. Such a simplified (and even tongue-in-cheek) scheme is offered, not with any intention of completeness, but to indicate in brief some of the radical rejections involved.

The ten commandments of radical postmodernism

1. *Thou shalt not worship reason.* Where modernity, from the excitement of new sciences, elevated instrumental or empirical reason to total prominence, and where Descartes advocated method, certainty and clear ideas, postmodernism becomes disenchanted with such overweening rationalism, and prefers what Vattimo has termed 'weak thought' – with its shyness about all truth claims. Similarly, according to the 'deconstruction' proposed by Jacques Derrida, all reality is like a text, open to a myriad of conflicting interpretations. Instead of the 'modern' assumption that objectively correct answers are possible, we are all caught in a 'prison house of language', where relativism replaces any rationally ordered world. Meaning, if it exists at all, is created by us and is always in flux. Science itself has abandoned the quest for verifiable certitudes and has become anti-representational, indeterminate and tentative.

2. *Thou shalt not believe in history.* With a philosopher such as Hegel, history takes over from 'nature' as the key category for understanding existence. Hence where modernity promoted a proud confidence that human beings could at last take history into their own hands, shaping it in line with various aims or visions, postmodernism speaks of the 'end of history', questioning all such large hopes, preferring to live without big goals, content with utility, communicability and an immediacy where there is not real past or future. Concerning history, as in other fields, models of determinacy give way to chance and indeterminacy.

3. *Thou shalt not place hope in progress.* Although modernity distrusted absolutes and authorities, it put trust in utopias of progress – what Francis Bacon has called the *regnum hominis* with its evolutionary hopes of overcoming evils and creating situations of happiness. Postmodernism is partly born of the disasters of this

century and abandons all such hopes as arrogant and dangerous. Instead it cultivates only the partial and the fragmentary.

4. *Thou shalt not tell meta-stories.*   In a similar way modernity lived out various mythic stories of human heroism, such as Prometheus stealing the fire of the gods; but postmodernism rejects 'meta-narratives' as 'logocentric', that is to say, deceived by the inevitable human urge to find one central meaning for existence and to express this meaning in some story form. In so far as Christian faith seems an example of a 'meta-narrative', it comes under critique from postmodernism as 'totalizing': claiming that it can encompass everything and offer meaning for everything.

5. *Thou shalt not focus on the self.*   Where modernity from the Renaissance to the Enlightenment gave birth to a new humanism, an exaltation of human beings at the centre of the universe, and stressing psychological identity or the self-contained individual as the measure of all things, postmodernism proposes the 'death of man', in the sense of a radical scepticism about subjective approaches and about the importance given to personality and self-consciousness in Western culture. The Cartesian notion of a sovereign rational subject seems like an infant's illusion of omnipotence.

6. *Thou shalt not agonize about values.*   Where modern philosophy – as in the case of Kant – put questions of morality and freedom in the foreground of thinking, and where lived modernity tended to be austere and even puritan in its style, postmodernism cultivates the spirit of both Dionysus and Narcissus: a spontaneous hedonism goes hand in hand with aesthetic expressions of autonomy. In this privatized age of immediacy and of images, moral responsibility is viewed as an illusion inherited from a different era. In its extreme form, life is valueless, moral absolutes are illusory, and freedom is only a game. No stable points of reference remain.

7. *Thou shalt not trust institutions.*   Where the long process of modernity saw the evolution of the modern democratic state and an increasing role for politics in society, postmodernism distrusts all institutions as manipulative forms of oppression by the powerful. Traditions are merely modes of ideology and control. Churches are

inevitably perceived as being part of the naive and authoritarian past.

8. *That shalt not bother about God.*   From the religious point of view, modernity gradually made atheism into a plausible philosophy, and for the first time in world history, this rejection of faith by intellectuals became a widespread stance among the educated classes. Postmodernism does not so much reject atheism as assume it, outgrowing its militancy about the 'death of God', and preferring a dismissiveness about the very question of transcendence. Immanence comes to be common sense and the need for religious searching disappears. If one must, one can speak of the divine, in the sense of transitory feelings of ecstasy. But beware of the illusory notion of 'presence': absence is all.

9. *Thou shalt not live for productivity alone.*   Sociological modernity involved an urbanized organization of life imposed by the Industrial Revolution. Against the priority given to systems of economic efficiency, a mechanical exploitation of people and of the earth, and the dominant logic of the left-hand brain, postmodernism protests in the name of randomness, aesthetic play, and a range of liberations associated with the right-hand brain. Work is replaced by shopping and the fetish of style.

10. *Thou shalt not seek uniformity.*   Culturally modernity was a relentless leveller, imposing a Western-style sameness, believing in universal or typical features of human behaviour, and being blind to local or unique traditions. Postmodernism has rediscovered 'difference' as a key value and relishes in the seeming anarchy of cultural diversity.

Apart from the final two responses listed, postmodernism in this presentation appears more destructive than constructive. Its critique tends to ignore the permanent achievements of modernity: the progress in quality of life due to science and technology, the deeper sense of human dignity associated with modern democracy and with historical consciousness, the many freedoms offered by changed social situations, the goals of emancipation and equality, the birth of quasi-universal education, the autonomy and rights of the individual as against the system – to mention some chief points of breakthrough. Hence 'postmodernism' risks throwing out baby with bath water, through not recognizing the enduring contributions to culture from the various 'modern' revolutions.

As mentioned at the outset, this theoretical 'postmodernism' seems less relevant to questions of faith than 'postmodernity' as a cultural mood of recent times. Where postmodernism tends to express itself in a series of nihilist doubts about 'modern' claims, cultural postmodernity can be seen as an attempt to purify the modern inheritance. It does not play down the shadow sides nor does it reject the great achievements; rather it seeks to discern the tone of our culture, allowing for the excesses and imbalances of modernity, but seeking a healing of wounds rather than a rejection of the whole legacy.

Postmodernity as a cultural sensibility

As already suggested, it is helpful to make a distinction between 'postmodernism', as an intellectual reaction against the excesses of 'modern' claims, and 'postmodernity' as a potentially more positive cultural mood of today. For some authors postmodernity entails a radical departure from modernity, but others prefer to speak of 'late modernity', thus stressing that we are in a more advanced and problematic stage of much the same historical process. Anthony Giddens, a Cambridge sociologist, argues that it is premature to label our age postmodern. He prefers to speak of 'high modernity' (or 'radicalised modernity') because 'the consequences of modernity are becoming more radicalised and universalised than before'.[3] Interestingly he sees the zone of inter-personal trust and self-disclosure as forced into prominence because of the lack of anchors in contemporary culture.

Indeed this highlighting of the personal was confirmed during a course I taught last year at the Gregorian University in Rome. I asked the students to pool their insights on the characteristics of modernity and postmodernity. I filled the board with the answers. They came up with all the stock descriptions of modernity, which fell into two families – one dealing with ideas and ideologies, and another focusing more on the individual self. Thus among the more theoretical characteristics of modernity we listed: new trust in rationality, in science, in progress, in human control over nature and history, and a parallel distrust of tradition and authority, leading to a spirit of revolution in politics and in the religious sphere the emergence of privatized faith and ultimately of 'modern' atheism. In the zone of the self modernity seemed marked by a primacy of individual dignity, personal rights, and autonomy of conscience, and therefore by a new sense of self-creative freedom in many fields.

An interesting trend emerged when we turned our attention to the characteristics of postmodernity. A whole series of question marks were placed against some achievements of modernity, as contradictions long present in the modern enterprise came more sharply into focus. Did not the exciting novelties of science become frozen into a dehumanizing of truth? Or the arrival of democracy sink into an anchorless liberalism? And so on. But then it became more than a matter of question-marks. Instead of having to write down new words on the board, all I had to do was draw a large X over various features of modernity. We ended up cancelling out all the non-personalist aspects of modernity. Thus, postmodernity looks with deep suspicion at an arrogant sense of reason, at scientism, or naive claims to progress, or insensitive dominance over the earth, or utopias about history. However, we did not put an X over the various forms of subjectivity fostered by modernity (nor over the related theme of rejection of authority). Instead, we discussed how in postmodernity the fate of the self deepens into a new isolation and loss of connections. And yet one of the surprises of postmodernity seems to stem from this loneliness and shows itself in an openness to spiritual searching. On the religious front, postmodernity, at least in some of its tendencies, is much less sure about atheism.

In short, the big claims of modernity have fallen under suspicion and come to be largely rejected, but the 'turn to the subject' born with modernity has not only survived the transition but become an even more crucial strand of our lived culture. It has given rise to a new sensibility that can be read either positively or negatively. According to one judgement we have fallen further into isolation, fragmentation and narcissism, where life is an indifferent game and individual options are merely aesthetic and provisional. But according to another reading, the oft-maligned sense of self can be the source of our hope, because permanent hungers of the heart come to expression with new honesty and the quest for liberation and authenticity takes on a new humility. Even the sense of dispersal, according to this interpretation, rebounds into a new spiritual search for community and roots. Spirituality becomes not just a fashionable term but a real issue in this era beyond the oppressions of modernity.

Modernity, we have seen, caused a fragmentation of three horizons: the sense of self, the sense of truth, the sense of God. The self became lonely, self-conscious and withdrawn (and in literature the novel is born to mirror a new social class and replace the more public genre of drama). Truth, measured mainly with the instruments of empirical science, also withdrew into the sphere of the verifiable. God, as imagined by the defenders of faith in the seventeenth century and later, retreated to theism and even deism: theologians become narrowly rational, forgetful of Christ, and leaving the field of spirituality to sentiment.[4] Even in that same period there was a resistance movement against the ravages of modernity: the pre-Romantic valuing of sensibility gave new depth and dignity to the lonely self, and Romanticism itself sought to save humanity from mere reason and the anonymous city – locating salvation within the world of imagination and feeling.[5]

Two poles of postmodernity

If all these forces were at work in modernity, not just as an ideology, but as an emerging sensibility, in a similar way we can identify two poles within postmodernity: it may reject the excessive certainties of modernity but not that second side of groping selfhood. Of course the most theoretical exponents of postmodernism voice scorn for humanism and the myth of the self. As distinct from the radical destroyers, postmodernity has its more hopeful purifiers. Instead of delighting to dance on the grave of modernity, these want to rescue it from its excesses and contradictions. From the point of view of religious faith, these less extreme postmoderns are potential dialogue partners for theology in its reflections on culture and faith.

The accompanying diagram tries to capture something of the polarities between theoretical and negative postmodernism (on

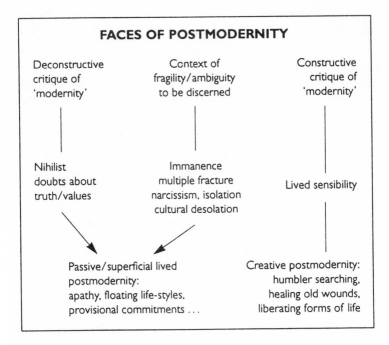

FACES OF POSTMODERNITY

| Deconstructive critique of 'modernity' | Context of fragility/ambiguity to be discerned | Constructive critique of 'modernity' |

Nihilist doubts about truth/values

Immanence multiple fracture narcissism, isolation cultural desolation

Lived sensibility

Passive/superficial lived postmodernity: apathy, floating life-styles, provisional commitments . . .

Creative postmodernity: humbler searching, healing old wounds, liberating forms of life

the left) and an emerging sensibility of postmodernity (on the right). If the left line starts as radical doubt, the right line represents a certain search for new hope. In between, there is the more ambiguous and less attractive face of postmodernity: the bored indifference that seems related both to the fragmentation of culture and to the more nihilist theorists. This version of lived postmodernity I call 'passive' or 'superficial' to distinguish it from the 'creative postmodernity' that, as will be seen, offers much more opportunity for dialogue with faith.

Creative postmodernity, in this way, is a new sensibility that aims at wholeness. It sees modernity as having caused an abyss between the rational and the subjective aspects of humanity, by developing both dimensions in isolation from one another. Postmodernity as sensibility is groping towards forms of life that bridge these divisions. Thus, where both reason and feeling suffered by being cut off from one another, the tendency of creative postmodernity is to overcome this 'dissociation of sensibility' (as T. S. Eliot once called it) by means of new connectedness and by revaluing holistic thinking.

Undoubtedly, one can find fragmentation, impotence and narcissism in the lived culture, but there is also a different searching beyond the old certitudes, including a new willingness to revisit the despised zones of the spiritual and the religious as roots of our healing. In the words of Charles Taylor, 'one has to see what is great in the culture of modernity, as well as what is shallow or dangerous'.[6] Thus postmodernity can mean a retrieval of resources neglected through the lopsided triumph of modernity – old anchors like community and spirituality.

If modernity involved separations of worlds, and if its lasting impact lies more in sensibility than in ideas or ideologies, then postmodernity may reopen doors because of its humbler recognition of wounds and wants. In this sense postmodernity would seem to be more friend than foe for religious commitment today. But before affirming that position too complacently, one has to face the objection that postmodernity – although less ideologically hostile to religion than modernity – is in fact more apathetic in its stance before possible religious faith.

Most commentators would agree that the postmodern self suffers from a new isolation. The old supports of a cohesive society have almost disappeared. The anchors in religious belonging have lessened drastically for many people. We live in the wake of multiple fracture, where the individual's various languages of searching are themselves cut off from one another. If this is so, then postmodernity – even in its lived or everyday forms – suffers from an incapacity for roots. This shows itself in the decline of social commitments concerning justice. It also shows itself in a diminished sense of the past, a kind of cultural amnesia. If this is valid, then judgemental 'isms' are unworthy: it is not just a question of narcissism, hedonism, nihilism, post-materialism and so on. It is a question of suffering sensibility, of lostness, of a handicapped quest within a culture that offers few connections with others or with history.

This picture seems at first to be a cultural desert. If faith, ever since we emerged from the easy inheritances of premodernity, has had to be a decision against the tide (as in the early centuries of Christianity), then this landscape seems even more a formula for paralysis. Because of such little cultural support and such little attractiveness in the mediations of religion, faith options become harder to reach, and when one adds in the pressures of trivial postmodernity, this faith dimension can often fade into unreality.

But everyone seems agreed, paradoxically, that a spiritual hunger is stronger than in modernity, more acutely so because of the new cultural desolation. The spiritual hunger is real but with so much religious rootlessness, there is a danger of ending up with a floating spirituality very far from the definiteness of Christian faith and one which can even be a form of postmodern unbelief. In spite of this ambivalence, there is a significantly new tone of religious openness. The theologian David Tracy has been concerning himself in recent years with the issue of postmodernity, stressing that it represents both a cultural and a theological category. He views postmodernity as a new sensibility, more open to religious horizons than during the long reign of modernity. He praises the key achievements of modernity – the philosophical maturity born from the crisis of the scientific revolution, the 'bracing honesty of an historical conscious-ness', the liberating aspects of the democratic ideal – and yet he discerns a dangerous levelling and pride within modernity, a 'drive to sameness, the modern Western scientific, technological, demo-cratic culture that *is* culture and history', the arrogance of modern liberalism that never says out loud but implies that 'Western culture *is* culture'.[7]

According to Tracy, it becomes possible to stress again the crucial frontiers between theology and spirituality. Modernity tended to reduce everything to external 'religion' or even to deism. Postmod-ernity is more open to the prophetic, the cosmological, and the mystical or participative dimensions of religious experience. A post-modern spirituality can be born that does justice both to core relationship of faith, the radical concreteness of Christ and his pro-phetic challenges for our broken worlds, and equally values the wise shyness of a negative theology, reticent to explain its mystery, or to name it too neatly, and above all suspicious of cheap words.

Towards a balance sheet

Perhaps there is a tendency to be too hard on modernity and too rosy about the more holistic sensitivity of postmodernity. Be that as it may, the case for a positive view of this new cultural mood is based on its double claim – to heal some of the wounds of modernity and to reopen neglected wavelengths of exploration. Where modernity left 'man' lonely and without purpose, postmodernity seeks to expand the set of relationships, cosmic and communitarian, and to reopen the conversation about the ultimate goals of life.

According to these more favourable interpretations, postmodernity is characterized by new sensitivities on three fronts: ecology, feminism and the return of spirituality. Indeed the three areas are deeply connected: they are rooted in a realization that our history has suppressed something precious, which now needs liberation. Modernity was exploitative of the earth and of peoples, forgetful of women and of the feminine in each person, and forced the spiritual dimension of life to retreat to the poetic and the private. If so, postmodernity proposes a series of openings. Already these three cultural horizons, that were not so strongly felt even a generation ago, together represent a major shift in sensibility. As regards feminism in particular, we can now see that much of the shadow side of modernity was androcentric; thus the roots of injustice to women and the roots of deafness of revelation were both legitimated by the lopsidedness of 'modern' culture. The masculinist and the atheist forms of arrogance were twins. Since postmodernity questions these versions of pride and prejudice, it opens new horizons for our self-imagining as women or men, and equally as potential hearers of the Word.

Some Spanish-language theologians seem to offer the most positive readings of postmodernity as a new sensibility, singling out several zones of purification and hope for faith:[8] the return of attention to religious experience, an area despised as illusory by modernity; a healthy distance between religion and manipulative or totalizing power systems, as fostered especially by liberation theologies; prophetic critique of the idols of theism (a first cousin of modernity) and of rationally packaged versions of God; a quest for more adequate wavelengths before divine mystery, shown in retrievals of negative theology or narrative theology; renewal in the aesthetic or festive or contemplative aspects of faith (even von Balthasar can be seen as postmodern in a certain sense); a Christianity that faces the challenge of differentness of cultures, overcoming modernity's suppression of this diversity; and while there are new risks of a narcissistic and 'light' religiousness within trivial postmodernity, there is the opposite tendency to trust the limited or fragmentary, and forge a more patient spirituality of option for the poor. Llano speaks of postmodernity as returning to an analogical way of thinking as a non-rationalist and gradualist approach to meaning, and in this he sees hope for linking *praxis* and *poeisis*, which had been long polarized in classical modernity. One finds something of the same 'friendly' diagnosis in Elizabeth Johnson who sees 'postmodern consciousness' as aware of 'the fragility of the human project' and yet prizing 'essential connectedness' and the 'importance of community'.[9] According to Elaine Graham, contemporary feminists have become acutely aware of the gender bias present in modernity; she hopes that postmodern theologies can ground themselves in 'performative' practices of faith-communities and in the process of transcendence disclosed in 'the encounter with the Other'.[10]

Some of these claims concern developments too recent for easy discernment. Some of them may prove short-term. And yet it is not just millennial enthusiasm that makes us think that we are at a major turning point in culture. Over against an intellectual postmodernism that views God as a 'phantom of grammar', there has arisen an alternative sensibility that sees such dismissiveness as simply 'tone-deaf': if it neglects 'music and the arts, without which human life might indeed not be viable', it is in danger of forgetting the significance of a whole range of human searching, its capacity for wonder and also for transcendence.[11] Beyond the tragedies and empty freedoms of modernity, a 'remarkable opening of the soul is taking place'; imaginative prophets like Dostoevsky or Solzhenitsyn, who have learned most from suffering, are postmodern in the sense of contemplating again 'the God who for so long has been displaced' from the centre of culture and consciousness.[12] In this way postmodernity becomes a movement of resistance to a long oppression of the spirit.

Hopes for creative postmodernity

Do we need yet another distinction, perhaps, between passive and creative postmodernity (as indicated at the bottom of the diagram)? Passive would point to the drifting nature of contemporary life-styles – what can be described as the 'alienated immediacy' of consumerist existence, or as the cultivated cynicism that reigns in sophisticated circles (echoing the more conscious negativity of postmodern*ism*). Whereas this passive postmodernity seems in continuity with the voids of modernity, and religiously is a form of apathy and distance from the hungers of faith, creative postmodernity questions all that long amnesia. It seeks to forge a new language of living for today. It reopens doors locked or at least neglected by modernity. It insists that there is more to life than the rational system or the dominance of technology. It hopes to find ways of healing our inherited forms of loneliness – all those separations of self from society, or reason from feeling, or science from religion, or man from woman, or theology from spirituality, or individual depth from embracing the struggles of history. Its tone is one of shy searching, of a healthy suspicion of systems and of easy certitudes. It is impressed more by praxis than by grand theorizing.

Put like this, it could seem another utopian agenda, doomed to disappointment. But there is a certain saving humility at the heart of this postmodernity that starts small, goes one step at a time, and values the limited horizon of the possible. With this qualification, disappointments can perhaps be avoided, because at its best it seeks to discern our needed liberations if we are not to suffer from new oppressions of our humanity and our imagination. This face of postmodernity – as distinct from the superficial styles or the nihilist militancy – can be a way of reclaiming a space for mystery after the waste lands of secular modernity.

Besides we need a postmodernity of our own Christian making. It is not a question of watching the signs of the times, hoping passively for a change in the weather, but rather of seeing that already this humbler moment after modernity is itself a friendly moment for creative communication of the Christian vision. Possibilities open up for probing a more genuine sense of self after identifying the damage of false individuality as proposed by hard modernity. Parallel possibilities open up to link this new search of the self with communitarian and spiritual horizons, in ways that have not been culturally credible for centuries. As John Haldane has argued, in order to go forward we also need to go back: 'a better postmodern future is to be found in the seriously recovered pre-modern past'.[13]

When the self is less lonely, when the culture finds its shared language of community on local and world level of justice, when theology finds common ground with spirituality, then we are talking about a new sensibility that is far from vague. It is a significant convergence of hungers and of potentials in need of discernment and inculturation – topics that are to be explored in subsequent chapters here.

Chapter Nine

Horizons of Inculturation

Only those who themselves have been resurrected can actually celebrate Easter. (Dorothee Soelle)[1]

To think that Christianity will not change a situation is to rob the Christian message of its most important part. (Robert Schreiter)[2]

Inculturation is a relatively new term for something with long roots in Christian history, even though that 'something' is lived with a different urgency and with more complex awareness in our day.[3] St Paul (as will be seen in more detail in the next section) underwent a significant conversion of attitude in Athens, and took a sympathetic step towards the culture of a city that previously had left him disgusted (Acts 17). The very fact that Christians have four gospels and not one is a powerful symbol of how preaching the good news was shaped from the beginning by the needs of different audiences or cultures. That the New Testament is written and comes down to us in Greek, and not in the language of Jesus himself, is an indication of a dramatic and painful decision by the early Christians – to reach out beyond Jewish circles to the huge culture of the Gentiles. Again one can point to the history of Christian art as showing how faith has sought out different changing mediations that mirror many shifts of sensibility through the centuries.

The best chapters of Church history constitute a long adventure of trying to make real, in new languages and cultures, the revelation of God's love in Jesus Christ. In fact, a famous Roman document of 1659, from the then recently founded Congregation for the Propagation of Faith, gave these blunt instructions for missionaries going to China:

Do not bring any pressure to bear on these people to change their manners, customs and practices, unless these are obviously contrary to religion and morality. There is nothing more absurd than to want to bring France to China – or to bring Spain or Italy or any part of Europe. Carry none of that but rather faith which neither despises nor destroys the way of life and the customs of any people, when these are not evil things. On the contrary, faith desires that these traditions be conserved and protected.[4]

A changed horizon

Why are we talking so much about inculturation in these last decades if such sensitivity to local culture was already, at least in wiser moments of Church history, a guiding ideal for evangelization? Because our new horizons of awareness force us to take the diversity of local cultures more seriously than in previous ages. In particular with the arrival of historical consciousness as one of the hallmarks of modern thought, it became impossible to think of any one culture as a permanent or perfect model of life. Once we see the extent to which our ways of thinking and acting are products of history, then we accept more easily the relativity of our languages of living the Christian vision.

Besides, this intellectual insight concerning plurality of cultures has been accompanied by the ending of many colonial regimes as well as by a globalization process in world communications. As a result the previously unchallenged culture of Europe has begun to see itself as no longer the classical way of 'civilization', something to be exported and even imposed on less 'advanced' cultures. Without denying the rich heritage of the West, and its unique role in Christian and world history during the millennium now ending, we need to confess the blind spots of that history: its colonial arrogance and violence, its assumption of inferiority in different ways of life, and its own internal lopsidedness of development (cultivating the scientific and the organizational, a 'masculinist' bias in interpreting life).

Certain forms of mission to foreign cultures are now seen to have been marred by bias – seeing the home language of Christianity as normality and tending to dismiss genuinely spiritual aspects of the receiving culture. The new awareness of inter-culturality offers mutual challenges and helps: in the mirror of 'difference' the previously complacent Western culture can recognize some of its own dehumanizing features, or in more Christian terms, the culture can repent of its own sinful structures and admit its need of conversion. What is meant by inculturation is the opposite of that previous insensitivity, but the word is not only awkward but potentially misleading. As Cardinal Ratzinger has put it, 'faith itself is culture', and because there is no such thing as 'pre-cultural or de-cultured Christianity', perhaps a better term would be 'inter-culturality' in order to highlight the 'meeting of cultures' entailed in evangelization.[5]

Ideally the gospel transcends all cultural embodiments but in reality a pure encounter with a culture-free gospel is impossible. Some theologians of inculturation talk as if there were an ahistorical 'essence of christianity' waiting to be incarnated, which 'is to ignore the fact that christianity never existed, not even in its first days, without being expressed in some cultural forms'; instead the adventure of Church history always means a 'meeting of cultures in search of a new and original expression of the one faith'.[6] From a different perspective, Christopher Dawson, historian of religion and culture, looked back at the interactions between faith and barbarianism in Europe in the first millennium and stressed that it was not a matter of easy 'assimilation and permeation, but rather one of contradiction'; interestingly, he added that the key factor in the conversion of the tribes was not the newness of Christian doctrine but the 'new power' of holiness transparent in monastic culture.[7]

Inculturation as crucial to evangelization

One could give a lot of space to the evolution of the term 'inculturation', tracing its different uses in anthropology and sociology. In those fields (leaving aside the possible distinctions between enculturation, acculturation and so on) the main interest has been in how people are 'socialized', in the sense of learning the ways of the group through a process of social formation. But the details of this background can be left aside because inculturation has now become a specifically theological term and one which stresses the reciprocal process involved in communicating the gospel across cultures. Just as the gospel casts new light on each human situation, those situations in turn can bring different dimensions of the gospel into new life.

When this term was adopted in Church discourse it was to emphasize that evangelization, echoing the Incarnation itself, demands the insertion of 'the Gospel into the very heart of culture and cultures'.[8] The need for a new, if controversial, term symbolized a new ambition concerning the communication of faith today: not simply adaptation of the language of preaching or worship to the people in question, not only the need for the missionary to understand the cultural context before seeking to communicate the gospel, not even the challenge for the agents of evangelization to immerse themselves and become genuinely at home in the receiving culture for faith, but rather a different set of sensitivities, priorities and goals in the process of evangelization.

This new emphasis, captured in the global term inculturation, was born – as already mentioned – from various contemporary insights: (a) a new awareness from anthropology of the dignity and diversity of cultures, (b) from a more developed theology of the presence and action of the Spirit in all cultures, and (c) a recognition that evangelization is a two-way process of double conversion or mutual enrichment; the faith horizon of the evangelizer is also transformed and challenged through contact with a different culture. All three elements entail a transcendence of attitudes of merely giving-and-receiving, or of more older pastoral strategies. A key hope is that evangelization can take place from *within* the culture being evangelized. Even before the term 'inculturation' was used in official Catholic statements, Pope Paul VI wrote in 1975 of evangelization as involving 'transforming humanity from within' (*Evangelii nuntiandi*, No. 18). Thus inculturation involves more than changing a receiving culture from outside: it implies that the gospel will be fully and permanently rooted only when it has been received, felt, celebrated and lived within the deep language of a local culture.

Obviously there is a certain diversity of emphasis within the literature on inculturation. In some theological commentators it can seem to be an ideal goal of integration to be sought and possibly never fully achieved. More often, however, it represents a means to an end, a dimension or stage within evangelization. For instance, the Catholic Bishops of Latin America at their Santo Domingo assembly in 1992 suggested a fourfold movement within which inculturation comes in third place: their text spoke of 'knowledge and discernment of modern culture with a view towards adequate inculturation' and of 'a true inculturation as a way to evangelize culture'.[9] Hence the phases of experience and sifting come first, followed by inculturation, and then the possibility of an evangelized culture. In this model inculturation is seen as a middle term and not an end in itself.

Fourfold theological foundation

If inculturation is an essential part of evangelization, it is because Christian faith is always more than a private or even personal truth: it is God's vision of way-truth-life, given through Christ in the reality of history. As such, faith is inseparable from a converted way of life in community and in history. Faith that does not promote a healed world remains dead. And if it were possible to have genuine faith in a merely personal way, regardless of society or history, then inculturation would never be necessary. But that kind of faith is not Christian. A faith that does not find shared language of living is a stunted faith: as already seen, a faith that does not 'become culture' is one that is 'not fully lived out'.[10]

In recent years it has become a common practice to link inculturation with four of the fundamental mysteries of faith – Creation, Incarnation, Redemption through the Paschal Mystery, and Pentecost. Scripture scholars now widely accept that the creation accounts in Genesis were shaped to counter Babylonian myths of origin during the period of the Exile. In other words those great narratives are early examples of dialogue between faith and culture. As against the Babylonian stories of conflict and chaos, Genesis shows God serenely and freely creating as a gift to humanity, and indeed portrays God as an artist rejoicing in the sheer goodness of the finished work. Besides, these texts are much more than stories of origin: they are rooted in a sense of God's continuing relationship with us in our responsibility for the earth, for each other, for human history itself.

Creation theology, in this light, is the basis for the long adventure of human culture – symbolized in the mandate to human beings to grow and rule the earth or in the act of naming all the animals (Gen. 1:28; 2:20). Thus there is a biblical foundation for seeing culture as *the* human response to God's continuing creative gift, as a co-operation through responsibility with the Creator in the whole complex challenge of history – becoming 'fellow-workers with God' (1 Cor. 3:9).

Theologically speaking, there is only one Creation; all other uses of the term are analogical. And yet culture – in the 'higher' sense of conscious spiritual exploration – has usually been viewed as creativity, and within the Christian tradition, as echoing the work of the artist-Creator. If God created all that is good, human culture at its best seeks to start from that gift and to build our world with the same freedom and love. Biblically, this is the ideal image, but even within the early chapters of Genesis shadows come, culture turns sour and the results are exile, violence and Babel. This radical ambiguity of human culture points forward to the relevance of the Redemption within the process of inculturation.

If Creation theology is vital for a biblical perspective on culture in general, the Incarnation of Jesus Christ is *the* theological basis for inculturation, and this parallel has often been highlighted in Church statements and by theologians. The first papal use of the term inculturation came in an address of John Paul II to the Pontifical Biblical Commission in 1979, when he spoke of this 'neologism' as expressing well an aspect of the 'great mystery of the Incarnation'. Therefore inculturation imitates, so to speak, that embracing of humanity by God in Christ, in order to give flesh to the gospel again in different cultures.[11]

In a 1995 document that emerged from the special Synod for Africa, entitled *Ecclesia in Africa*, the Pope expands more than in any previous statement on the theological foundations of inculturation, pondering the three mysteries of Incarnation, Redemption and Pentecost.[12] He speaks of the Incarnation of the Word as 'a mystery which took place in *history*, in clearly defined circumstances of time and space, amidst a people with its own culture'; later he stresses that because the Incarnation 'was complete and concrete [it] was also an incarnation in a particular culture' (No. 60).

From this analogy with the humanity of Christ comes a theological confidence to appreciate particular cultures as potential languages for the Word; if cultures need Christ for their fullness, in another sense Christ needs cultures in order to continue and complete the gift of the Incarnation in different contexts of history. More pastorally, the Incarnation parallel offers a double challenge to the evangelizer – to practise a similar self-emptying and to enter fully into the cultural realities of people whom one wishes to evangelize.

But if inculturation is, in the light of the Incarnation, a challenge to the evangelizers, there is another aspect, rooted rather in the mystery of the Redemption, where the process of inculturated evangelization must become a challenge to the 'receiving' culture as well. In this way two elements will be in healthy tension in any process of inculturation: an embracing of human realities and a purification of dehumanizing aspects of the culture from within. In the words of *Ecclesia in Africa*, inculturation, which involves both 'insertion' and 'transformation' (No. 59), must 'follow the "logic" proper to the Mystery of the Redemption': every culture 'needs to be transformed by Gospel values in the light of the Paschal Mystery. It is by looking at the Mystery of the Incarnation and of the Redemption that the values and counter-values of cultures are to be discerned' (No. 61). This more prophetic note in the chord of inculturation seeks to do justice to the presence of evil in human history, and to the long struggle of each culture towards Christian authenticity.

Without this link with the Cross and Resurrection of Jesus, inculturation could remain naively optimistic, or merely a call for more respectful insertion in a given milieu, making oneself all things to all people in order to save them in Christ (cf. 1 Cor. 9:22). In the light of the Redemption inculturation reveals its inevitably conflictual side: culturally entrenched structures of sin are always in need of recognition and of liberation.

One of the imbalances in discussing inculturation is that sometimes the term is so identified with a positive Incarnation-emphasis that it comes to mean an entry into cultures without much reference to their transformation. This can be due to a bending-over-backwards that becomes an 'over-estimation of culture';[13] if so, a certain 'cultural romanticism' creeps in, whereby traditional cultures seem beyond critique and the inevitable tension between the Incarnation and Redemption dimensions becomes suppressed. The ever-difficult harmony between these two aspects was expressed in an influential description of inculturation offered by Pedro Arrupe, General of the Jesuits, in 1978:

> Inculturation is the incarnation of christian life and of the christian message in a particular cultural context, in such a way that this experience not only finds expression through elements proper to the culture in question (this alone would be no more than a superficial adaptation), but becomes a principle that animates, directs and unifies the culture, transforming and remaking it so as to bring about 'a new creation'.[14]

Pentecost and plurality

That last expression leads naturally to the fourth analogy – Pentecost. In the comment of *Ecclesia in Africa*, 'all the peoples of the earth ... profess in their own tongue the one faith in Jesus' as 'the Spirit, who on the natural level in the true source of the wisdom of peoples, leads the Church with a supernatural light into knowledge of the whole truth' (No. 61). There are three main points here: inculturation seeks to echo the miracle of unity in diversity; the Spirit has already been at work in cultures – even before the coming of evangelization; the Church brings a gift and receives a gift in the process of inculturation.

Pentecost symbolizes, in other words, the beginning of a new unification under the Spirit, and instead of the division of Babel, there becomes possible a different relationship between previously fragmented cultures. It is also the moment of the birth of the missionary Church, symbolized by an extraordinary reaching into the languages of diverse cultures.

In line with this Pentecost analogy one can also reflect on the challenge of today's pluralism of culture. As long ago as the mid-sixties Karl Rahner argued that 'faith has a history of its own, because the absolute self-revelation of God ... necessarily includes the unlimited possibility of acceptance in a variety of ways'. In other words, every culture and every age in order to remain 'true to the primitive truth' has in fact to 'discover a new form'. It is of the very nature of Christianity to evolve 'the most diverse forms of faith' because of 'widely differing cultures', and there is no guarantee that well-intentioned believers will always arrive at the 'form of faith which is most suitable'.[15] In Rahner's view, faith risks self-destruction if it fails to create the forms of faith demanded by a new culture. Long before the term 'inculturation' came into common use, he was pointing to its necessity not just for pastoral reasons but because the dialogue between God's Word and human response always takes place within the flux of history. The ultimate goal of inculturation is reached when a culture is capable of 'self-theologizing' and of embodying faith within its own symbolic forms.[16]

Relevant to the post-Christian world?

The avalanche of writing on inculturation within the last two decades has brought out both an old simplicity and a new complexity. It is simple because, at bottom, evangelization means seeking to reach people's hearts as shaped by the cultures around them. It is complex because so much is entailed in this slow process of pastoral imagination. That complexity is due to various key factors that have come more into focus with the years and which can be listed here by way of conclusion.

1.   Cultural consciousness: awareness of the omnipresence of cultural factors fosters a sense of urgency and of delicacy about the goal of evangelizing not only individuals but the cultures they inhabit.

2.   Universality of the Spirit: a broader theology of divine action in history gives rise to reverence for the goodness present in all cultures and a hope to discern the presence of grace in the lived values and symbols of each people.

3.   The challenge of reciprocal discovery: as against the older model of preachers and pagans, the trans-cultural communication of Christian faith can offer new light on the gospel vision to both 'givers' and 'receivers'.

4.   Conversion of horizons: inculturated evangelization cannot

avoid some clash with elements of deception and superficiality that afflict all cultures.

5. The local community: the crucial search for authentic forms of Christian life takes place within the concrete situation of each people.

The debates around the topic of inculturation have inevitably been focused on non-Western situations. That is where the issue posed itself most urgently. Does this mean that it is of little or no significance for the so-called Christian West? On the contrary, inculturation is as relevant to First-World countries 'which have been Christianized and now de-Christianized, as it is to the cultures of the Third world in which the Gospel has only recently been proclaimed'.[17] John Paul II has spoken of inculturation as 'the heart, the means and the objective of the new evangelization' (a goal mainly linked to the secularized West).[18] Inculturation therefore needs a difficult retranslation – one might say reinculturation – for the more secularized situations of the Western world. In these post-Christian contexts an 'inculturated evangelization' has the pastoral goal 'to introduce the possibility and reality of God through practical witness and dialogue'.[19]

The same insights apply that have been found necessary in more 'missionary' contexts: the need for sensitivity in reading the hungers of this seemingly secular culture; a trust that the Spirit is at work even in this difficult moment of Church history; the quest for appropriate languages of faith to meet the spiritual sensibility of postmodernity; discernment of the various Areopagi of culture in the West; a realization that mature faith has to root itself within the life-styles of today; at the same time the gospel has to challenge and transform what is sinful within the dominant culture. In short, the three key invitations of Church discourse on this issue have to be imagined anew within the complex cultural context of the West: inculturation of the gospel (initially a challenge to the Church to forge fresh embodiments of faith in tune with people today); evangelization of culture (the other side of the coin, whereby the culture itself is challenged into greater authenticity); faith becoming culture (the creation of communities of reflection and commitment that incarnate Christian models of faith for now).

Chapter Ten

Cultural Discernment

> *We can simultaneously feel bound to plod round the cultural treadmill
> yet also brim over with criticism and creativity.* (Margaret Archer)[1]

> *The basic problem with the consumer society is not that it makes us
> desire too much, but that it makes us desire too little. We are distracted
> from our true freedom.* (Tony Kelly)[2]

Towards the end of *Pride and Prejudice* Jane Austen offers a beautifully barbed critique of nominal Christianity. It occurs when Mr
Bennet is reading out a letter from Mr Collins. This social climbing
clergyman is complaining that Mr Bennet had received his daughter
under his roof even though she had been involved in an irregular
relationship: 'You ought certainly to forgive them as a christian, but
never to admit them in your sight, or allow their names to be
mentioned in your hearing'. This provokes Mr Bennet to exclaim
ironically, '*That* is his notion of christian forgiveness!'

It seems a good example of how a culture of respectability can
emasculate Christianity, making it fit the common sense of a social
group. When that happens the gospel vision becomes 'acculturated'
instead of 'inculturated'. Mr Collins is not alone in reducing the grit
of the Sermon on the Mount to the bias of the tribe. Small though
the example is, it seems typical of many cultural forms of pride and
prejudice that dilute Christian praxis and can underlie anything
from ordinary egoism to structural injustice or even violence. One is
forced into a certain humility about the large goals of 'inculturation'
or 'faith becoming culture'. 'Evangelization of culture' comes to
seem an uphill struggle in each particular moment of history and
indeed in each individual life.

One of the pitfalls in talking about faith-and-culture is that the
wavelength can remain serenely distant from reality. It can indulge
in vast generalizations or in optimistic visions of synthesis. It can

express huge hopes and ideals. And these balloon-like discourses need to be humbled by a blunt 'so what?' How are we to live wisely as Christians within the pressures and complexities of contemporary culture? In raising this question these final chapters approach some of the practicalities of the field, not so much in terms of plans for local action (by their nature they need local knowledge) but by focusing on basic attitudes and options.

The Italian writer and film director Pier Paolo Pasolini once suggested that in modern culture the Church should go into opposition, much like a political party that loses an election after a long time in power. The question here is about the tone of the opposition. In what spirit should faith view a dominant culture that, either openly or more silently, denies many of the values that are at the core of the Christian vision? The area of disposition is fundamental for discernment, and this chapter will offer variations on the question of how to discern culture.

Unbelief as a cultural product

First, however, it may help to identify some of those blockages to Christian faith that arise within contemporary culture. Years ago I advanced a thesis that has an attractive alliteration: in terms of psychological roots, unbelief takes three main forms – alienation, anger and apathy.[3] That appeared true of the seventies. But now in the nineties anger is rare; alienation seems in decline; and apathy has come to be the dominant type of unbelief in the Western world. Both anger and alienation are less because they both imply some Church contact from which to be alienated or against which to be angry! And there is now a whole new generation of baptized young adults whose formative experiences with religion or Church are so thin as to be almost non-existent. Rahner used to speak of 'anonymous Christians'; now we might better speak of 'anonymous unbelievers'. In the words of a Spanish theologian, at present the very 'question of God remains something irrelevant, or even nonexistent for the great majority of people. God is missing but is not missed. This is a genuinely new situation, which never existed before in the world'.[4]

What emerges is that, especially in younger generations, unbelief has become an inherited confusion, a distance from roots, an unaggressive puzzlement about religious practices and their language. As a result they experience unbelief as a cultural by-product. This is no longer de Lubac's 'drama of atheistic humanism' but rather an undramatic limbo of non-belonging. Such a contemporary sense of absence of faith, and the foreignness of its language, is captured in a powerful satiric poem by the Australian James McAuley who evokes a whole generation of the religiously 'disinherited':

> Who do not think or dream, deny or doubt,
> But simply don't know what it's all about.[5]

And yet is apathy the whole story now? Even if many young people remain victims of a certain cultural mood, others are moving not only beyond anger but beyond apathy. They may represent a new sensibility of spiritual searching that, as has been seen, is a surprising strand of our postmodernity. The appearance of apathy may be only a mask that conceals a disappointed hunger, but a hunger that is less shy to seek some nourishment and expression than decades ago.

Four forms of cultural unbelief

With this general background, there seem to be four main groupings of culturally rooted unbelief: religious anaemia; secular marginalization; anchorless spirituality; and cultural desolation. The first three can be described briefly but the fourth, as a gateway into the major theme of discernment, will need more attention.

'Religious anaemia' covers the many versions of distance from traditional Christian roots, where the fault for the malnutrition lies in a lack of pastoral imagination by the evangelizing or educating community. There is not so much a generation gap as a credibility gap of languages, where the typical mediations of Church can be experienced as a foreign tongue. Much discourse about evangelization may assume the presence of preambles of attitude or disposition that can no longer be taken for granted but have to be created and awoken. In short, religious anaemia is produced when the receiver encounters only the conventional or complacent externals of an institution, and when the communicators of faith fail to enter respectfully into the culture of the receiver.

Turning to 'secular marginalization': during a Plenary Assembly of the Pontifical Council for Culture in 1994, more than one speaker noted a new fear that the faith dimension cannot easily make itself heard in any public debate today and that there is a growing tendency to equate democracy with secular liberalism. Especially in the academic and media worlds, a secular culture reigns with the result that religion is subtly ignored as unimportant or as merely a private taste like classical music. Culturally this marginalization causes a collapse of 'plausibility structures'; as a result a whole interpretation of life comes to appear unreal or intellectually unworthy of serious attention.[6]

What can be called 'anchorless spirituality' points in an opposite direction and is one of the surprises of postmodernity – the so-called return of the sacred. When people find themselves 'sated but unsatisfied' by the old materialism, as well as bored or untouched by their experience of Church, they can enter a new search without anchors. It is that drifting that constitutes a danger: the hunger is good but insofar as the lived culture weakens people's Christian roots, such a spiritual quest leaves itself open to becoming a mixture of ancient heresies like gnosticism and pelagianism. In a context of religious malnutrition, such lonely spirituality easily becomes another form of dechristianization. Without community and contemplation, it risks being a narcissism without Christ. In fact this phenomenon seems the product of the two elements already described: where Church discourse fails to connect with human needs and where culture gradually forces religious consciousness into the realm of the private, then fundamental spiritual hungers in people remain unsupported and yet desperate in their longing for some kind of food. Thrown back on their own resources, people express their suppressed religiousness in different ways which can range, depending largely on temperament, from so-called New Age explorations to more fundamentalist rigidities.

The fourth diagnostic is 'cultural desolation', and the key words here will be disposition, imagination and freedom. The main thesis is that the pressures of the dominant culture leave many people blocked in a cultural desolation on the level of disposition or readiness for faith. Why? Because it kidnaps their imagination in trivial ways and therefore leaves them unfree for Revelation – or more precisely, for the hearing from which faith comes (cf. Romans 10:17).

Some people bemoan that schools or parishes are not teaching people the catechism any more, and that young people leave their education without clear notions of the meaning of Christian faith or Church worship. The point has some validity, but is weakened if it implies an exclusively conceptual version of truth, forgetting the impact of a certain cultural conditioning on the level of freedom of disposition rather than doctrine. Hence a first task in this situation is a ministry of disposition, an awakening of the hungers to which the truth may eventually be seen as answer. In this spirit William Barry warns that the 'influence of culture on us escapes our consciousness' and that we need to find 'how any of us encultured human beings can become free enough from our culture to be believers'.[7]

If the main faith blockages today come from cultural desolation on the level of disposition or readiness for faith, how can we help people towards that consolation or openness where faith can be born? It will mean liberating levels of hearing and of desire that become stifled in the everyday culture. The surrounding culture can be 'dia-bolic' or 'sym-bolic', in the sense of divisive and degrading, or else uniting human potentials into 'togetherness and community'.[8] Before the positive liberation of wonder, a certain negative clearing of the ground may be required. Religious education, for instance, needs to become counter-cultural, in the sense of helping students to identify the dehumanizing factors present in life-styles and assumptions of the culture. To be a Christian today means opting for a certain resistance movement, distancing oneself from the diminished life on offer in the dominant images around. But we need a note of caution here about the tone of our judgements. Too often we can fall into mere moaning about 'isms' (materialism, hedonism, immanentism . . .). Real Christian critique is more than generalized moaning. Discernment is concrete and ultimately positive – in search of genuine life.

It is worth recalling that Cardinal Newman always insisted that unbelief arises not from the intellect but from the state of one's heart, and that the crucial battle zone for faith or unbelief lies in the imagination. In his *Grammar of Assent* he wrote: 'the heart is commonly reached not through the reason, but through the imagination', adding with typical understatement, 'no man will be a martyr for a conclusion'.[9] As a similar comment on modern culture I value a statement of some fifty years ago by the poet T. S. Eliot: 'The trouble of the modern age is not merely the inability to believe certain things about God which our forefathers believed, but the inability to feel towards God and man as they did.'[10] This also locates the crisis not in creeds but in sensibility or imagination; it suggests that we have not so much a crisis of faith in the sense of a crisis of creed or message, as a crisis in the *language* or mediations of faith. It is on the pre-conceptual level of intuitive activity – called imagination – that religious meaning is encountered and explored. Indeed 'primordially religion is a function of the creative imagination'.[11]

In this light my thesis about cultural desolation and a resultant lack of freedom for faith situates itself on the level of sensibility. The secular rhythms of culture can kidnap the human imagination into an incapacity to attend to the call of God. The cultural messages embodied in the images around us enter the imagination unnoticed and become assumptions about reality that cause what Buber called an 'eclipse of God'. Thus the disposition or desire for faith becomes stifled through cultural desolation. Perhaps secularism has its most subtle victories in the battleground of imagination – not through outright militancy or violent assault but rather a hijack of the heart into secondaries.

Some commentators propose a more forceful role for theology within this contemporary situation: it should be more confident of itself as 'a social science', indeed as having the ability to save our culture from nihilism. However, it will do this not simply in theory but rather by linking 'logos' and 'praxis' in ways that restore 'freshness and originality' to the life-forms of Christian faith as alternatives to the cultural desolations around. Only if a 'distinctive practice' can be elaborated, and only if Christianity breaks out of the privatized models that it retreated to under the pressures of modernity, is there real hope for forging living forms of Christian culture today.[12]

Three Christian responses to culture

If the context is problematic in these ways, how is a Christian to respond wisely to such cultural confusions and pressures? Nobody can answer this question without acknowledging the classic work of H. Richard Niebuhr, entitled *Christ and Culture*, with its five models of relationship between faith and culture.[13] However, for present purposes I propose three schools of Christian response to culture: tense hostility; innocent acceptance; discernment and creation of culture. Indeed all three voices may echo within each of us at different times.

Hostility towards the culture

The first tendency – the tense adversary – is one of strongly negative judgement often allied to militant tone. Hamlet-like, this approach sniffs out 'something rotten in the state' of contemporary society and would voice its judgements something like this:

'The culture is simply sick. Trying to view it positively leads only to false compromises. We have lived too long in silence, fearing to speak out about the false turnings in cultural history. A Christian has to be radically suspicious of the deceptions entrenched in such value-shaping worlds as academic life, international politics, the economic system, or the entertainment industry. They are secularist and manipulative to the core, even when they pay lip-service to religious values or to individual freedom. Therefore believers have to protect themselves from cultural pollution by maintaining strong Church loyalty as a defence against these invading worlds of super-ficiality. Only from such a position of clear identity and difference will they have the authority needed to speak the truth and – even though faith is by its nature in perpetual opposition – also to begin a mission to convert the victims of this culture. Against its damage and multiple fracture, believers have to seek their true identity within the Church, in order to survive this sophisticated version of the dark ages.'

It is impossible to deny the grounds for such an evaluation. The danger lies less in the content than in the tone or in the strong possibility that the hostility is born of fear. Not that all Christian discourse must be meek and gentle, but rather that it has to be honest about the possible desolation behind such dismissiveness. The difficulty with these armour-plated Christian attitudes towards culture is a question of roots and of fruits. If the roots lack genuine listening or love for the situation of people, the fruits will be unproductive, and religion can even come to sound like fanaticism. Even if evils exist in the culture, sulking and sniping are unworthy as Christian responses. They often go hand in hand with a separatist tendency to construct a fortress of Church righteousness. Such negative attitudes are understandable as forms of panic and as efforts to identify the chaos of today in the light of God's revelation and judgement, but they are flawed insofar as they are grounded in a non-sympathy for the entire culture of now. Thus these voices become merely prophets of gloom – a category that Pope John XXIII chided, firmly and even humorously, at the opening of the Second Vatican Council, suggesting that he had to listen to too many diatribes about the modern world:

> In the daily exercise of our pastoral office, we sometimes have to listen, much to our regret, to voices of persons who, though burning with zeal, are not endowed with too much sense of discretion or measure. In these modern times they can see nothing but prevarication and ruin. They say that our era, in comparison with past eras, is getting worse, and they behave as though they have learned nothing from history, which is, none the less, the teacher of life ... We feel we must disagree with those prophets of gloom, who are always forecasting disaster, as though the end of the world were at hand. In the present order of things, Divine Providence is leading us to a new order of human relations.[14]

Innocent acceptance of the culture

The opposite tendency is to be so naive about culture as to be practically unaware of its dangers; it can be recognized in at least three forms – passive resignation, thoughtless secularization, and indiscriminate embracing of pluralism.

To fall into passive resignation means to abandon any attempt to influence the culture or to create alternatives. This position might well share some of the negative judgements of the 'adversary' position but instead of attacking, it tends to throw in the sponge about making any impact on the surrounding world. Everything seems so complex that one cannot hope to make any difference, and hence it seems wiser to cultivate one's own back garden, so to speak. This means retreating into non-contact with the culture, leaving that culture unchallenged in its control of people's imaginations and hearts.

Another possible version of this acceptance of the culture involves an unreflected 'buying into' the dominant values. Looking back now at some of the 'renewal' of religious life or of liturgy that took place in the decade after the Second Vatican Council, it can be asked whether it did not embrace a certain secularization too rapidly. In those overdue and necessary efforts at pastoral relevance, one could hold that valuable aspects of tradition were unwisely discarded. Even to raise this issue can seem 'restorationist', as if wanting to put the clock back. But it need not be so. In the urgency to emerge from the excessively closed culture of pre-conciliar Catholicism, a certain 'acculturation' seems to have taken place: the influence of the secular liberalism of the sixties caused such an unbalanced emphasis on individual expression that genuine elements of Christian anthropology were abandoned. It is not just a superficial question of religious dress or of folk music in the liturgy: these are transitory and secondary issues. More serious was an undervaluing of symbolic languages for the sacred or an insensitivity to the need for some counter-cultural structures if spirituality is to survive. Ultimately at stake was the inescapable differentness of the gospel way: it transcends common sense, challenges all merely human values to conversion and creates an inevitable tension with the assumptions of a non-religious culture. In this light some of the undiscerning assimilation of the anti-structural, anti-symbolic and anti-spiritual culture of the sixties now seems to be an example of 'innocent acceptance'.

A third source of weakness before the dominant culture comes from certain interpretations of 'pluralism'. Plurality of life-styles and meanings exists all around us and pluralism is a response to that complex reality. A valid pluralism recognizes the rights of other people even if it does not necessarily agree with their values. But some versions of cultural pluralism do not grasp that distinction and hence the values themselves topple over into relativism. If 'one culture is as good as the next', then there is no need for discernment of cultural practices.[15] An indiscriminate pluralism would abdicate any possibility of evaluating cultures. Its mistake is to slide from an acknowledgement of diversity and of rights to freedom into a hazy attitude whereby all cultural embodiments are equally valuable in their own way. But is it true? This soft kind of pluralism usually goes hand in hand with a 'coherence' rather than a 'referential' theory of truth; if there is only 'truth-within-a-system', then we have no yardstick for cultural discernment.

Discernment of dispositions

It is healthy, if somewhat uncomfortable, to look into these mirrors of naive anger or naive liberalism; it prepares the ground for a more genuine discernment of culture and shows that we need another wavelength of response. In this respect one can ponder the most relevant moment in the New Testament for this whole theme. Chapter 17 of the Acts of the Apostles offers a classic case of contrasting responses to the surrounding culture. St Paul's discourse on the Areopagus is often cited as the greatest New Testament example of a positive outreach to pagan culture and of the possible harmony between human aspirations and the revelation-event of Jesus Christ. But what is less frequently noted is that the generosity of his speech differs greatly from his own initial reactions to Athens. The account of his stay in the city begins with an unusually strong expression of negativity: 'his whole soul was revolted at the sight of a city given over to idolatry' (Acts 17:16). Indeed the Lucan introduction goes out of its way to stress the difficulties of reaching such a sophisticated but superficial culture, one that sneered at Paul as a 'parrot' and indulged itself in the latest ideas on the level of fads and mere entertainment.

It is all the more remarkable, therefore, that the Areopagus speech should open by praising the Athenians for being so religious and that Paul should now interpret an altar to an Unknown God, not as idolatry, but as a sign that the Athenians had genuine religious hungers and were worshipping God without fully knowing the One whom Paul came to announce. The remainder of his speech continues to obey the pastoral principle of making himself 'all things to all' types of people in order to reach them with the good news (1 Cor. 9:22). He gradually moves from external images to evoke the transcendence of God beyond all images. He gives special attention to the fundamental human experience of desire for God: people feel their way towards God, whereas in fact God is not far from anyone because in God 'we live and move and exist' (Acts 17:28). That last phrase is borrowed from a Greek poet – yet another symbol of the effort to enter into the culture and to invite people to faith from within their deepest values. Paul then seeks to move on from evoking human awe before creation to the need for repentance as the only way to leave ignorance behind. Of course this attempt at reaching Athenian culture ends in relative failure. People laugh at the mention of resurrection from the dead, but some postpone judgement, promising to hear him again, and some are converted. Indeed the text gives their names as if to highlight that fact.[16]

Paul's change of attitude from disgust with the culture to identifying seeds of the gospel within pagan religiousness seems a perfect example of the contrast between desolation and consolation that underlies all discernment. Contact with a new culture can easily provoke judgemental and negative reactions. Differentness causes fear. The externals may seem decadent. The behaviour of people can appear superficial and astray. But does that judgement stem from a certain desolation of attitude, a distrusting that the Spirit could be present within this cultural situation in any way? If so, the freedom to discern is not yet present. How did Paul move from disgust to generosity? Perhaps he prayed as he climbed the hill to the Areopagus. At all events he arrived at a more positive intuition into the values of Athenian culture. Behind the frivolous appearances lay deeper spiritual hungers. Behind the games of argumentativeness lay a poetry and a spirituality that he began to appreciate in a new way. Paul's whole disposition seemed to have undergone a sea change; such a graced conversion of attitude is a key to any Christian discernment of culture. We need to move from desolation of judgement to a discernment rooted in consolation. Otherwise we are in danger of seeing only the 'flatter and shallower forms' all too visible around us, and miss the 'higher and fuller modes of authenticity' that are also present as key characteristics of our culture.[17]

Discernment, in short, is a specifically spiritual and Christian way of reading reality. It aims at more than a human sifting of the shadows and lights in a social environment. Discernment does not neglect any human instruments for cultural analysis but it seeks to recognize the presence of the Spirit within the human. It enlarges the method of 'reading' a situation from description of outer factors to reflection on the deeper attitudes or dispositions of people. If the Spirit is at work, then the fruits will show themselves. Towards what are our hearts moving? That is a key question for spiritual discernment. It asks about the directional flow of our lives: is the culture leading us towards what is profoundly humanizing and creative of love, or pushing us towards what is imprisoning, destructive, and closed to compassion? One direction of flow is called consolation, the other desolation. Consolation therefore is not just a matter of 'feeling good' or of cultivating 'positive thinking'; it is a faith-based experience, a sense of expanding in harmony with what is deepest in us, the Spirit in us. In large options and in small reactions, consolation is an experience of being-in-tune-with-Christ. Desolation is the contrary experience of disharmony, disconnection, distance, distrust perhaps of everything and everyone. Consolation is like open hands, ready to receive. Desolation is like closed fists, ready to reject.

To practise this specifically Christian way of reading cultures involves a major shift of agenda from mere analysis of external influences and trends. It aims at a discerning of the dispositions the culture provokes in us and in others. Earlier I stressed cultural desolation as a source of blockage against faith for many people today. But faced with the sheer weight of that desolation around us, agents of the gospel may fall into a different desolation of response. Beyond mere hostility and beyond naive acceptance, there is the call to discern the culture with consolation, to move like St Paul from understandable disgust to a disposition of hope, rooted in the Spirit.

Without such a starting point in consolation, one is in danger of rejecting entire ways of life as utterly beyond the reach of the gospel. Of course negative judgement may be an appropriate response to important aspects of the dominant culture. The call to ground oneself in a certain consolation does not close the door to prophetic denunciation of what may be dehumanizing. Paradoxically we need to be able to see the desolations induced by the culture while guarding consolation as the ground of our Christian response, because to see desolation only with desolation is a formula for negativity. If that happens, one can become incapable of discerning any seeds of goodness. Indeed St Paul's initial reaction to Athens may well have been an example of viewing outer desolation with inner desolation.

So there can be no real discernment of culture without consolation as basic attitude, as a tone and trust that liberates our disposition to understand with something of the wisdom of God. Consolation does not mean rose-tinted viewing. In fact in involves a double expectation: there will be conflict, ambiguity, anti-values enthroned, but there will also be signs of hope and of real hunger, fruits of the Spirit. No situation is beyond redemption. Judge we must, but in a spirit of discernment, even of aggressive discernment, but never in a tone of dismissiveness. Some negative evaluations are inevitable – otherwise we would be innocent about evil and oppression. But blanket dismissals of contemporary culture seem both wrong and useless.

Discernment of culture, then, hinges on one's own spiritual disposition, and the resultant tone of one's dialogue with the culture. If desolation rules, a fairly fruitless tone of blanket moaning about reality can take over. If consolation is arrived at, critique of the falsities of the culture will be expressed in concrete ways, accompanied by a trust that these shadows are not the whole story: consolation means acknowledging that there are also authentic values within the culture which need liberating from the deceptions. Consolation breaks the negative magnifying glass that can only see decadence or disaster. Consolation is like that moment at the end of John's gospel where the disciples recognize the Lord on the shore after a night of total failure. Consolation is what liberated St Paul to glimpse the spirituality hidden behind the idolatry. In other words, consolation trusts that God is already present and somehow creative in all human cultures: therefore 'we are in consolation when we are fully in touch with what God is doing in our hearts' and when we try to 'bring to light the character of God's activity in those cultures' where we minister.[18] Discernment ultimately means sharing that conversion of disposition of St Paul in Athens, and thus being able to recognize smoke signals of hope rising from what may at first seem like a burnt-out desert.

Chapter Eleven

Cultural Consciousness in Ministry

Whence do we receive these Christian spectacles through which we inspect the world and ourselves? From Christ? No, from a Christian culture that is now passing away. (Sebastian Moore)[1]

The current challenge in youth ministry is not religious but anthropological: it is about who they are becoming. This question of identity requires a prior critique of the manipulative images in the dominant culture. (Riccardo Tonelli)[2]

A certain agreement seems to exist among sociologists about the spiritual identikit picture of young people in Europe and North America now. They present the young person of today as living within a restricted horizon of meaning and values. The typical quest is subjective rather than political, within the private sphere of relationships rather than in the larger world of commitments or projects. The 'drivers' or goals remain largely pragmatic and consumeristic – a good job, the freedom that comes with money to spend. For a generation that lacks models to follow, an adolescent phase of non-commitment can now extend itself well into their twenties. In other ways too a psychology of 'weakness' seems to be pervasive, in the sense of feeling themselves impotent before the large forces that govern society. This tendency to abdicate from large issues or to withdraw into a narcissistic space goes hand in hand with relativism over truth and morality. Truth becomes immanent – what-makes-sense-to-me, and conscience is viewed as infallible, in the sense of whatever feels 'OK' to the isolated individual. Some new spiritual searching marks a minority of young people, but often opting for unusual paths outside Christianity. Institutions, like churches or governments or educational systems, are generally viewed with considerable suspicion or indifference, seldom as sources of challenge or of life.

But to say all this is only half the story. To accept such a description of a generation is to forget that these trends do not happen without cause. Behind the present confusion and adriftness lies a culture of images that has educated this age-group more powerfully than at any previous time in history. It is one thing to put together elements of such an identikit picture. It is another, and more urgent, task to discern the roots of these characteristics in the pressures of a culture. More important still is to find ways of liberating people from the imprisonment of living as passive products of this culture. Insofar as they buy into the surrounding norms they become handicapped: victims of their environment, increasingly incapable of questioning the assumptions they have unconsciously absorbed from their environment.

The Cinderella story of the emergence of culture from obscurity into centre stage is echoed in a particular way in the field of youth ministry. Indeed, without alertness to the cultural context, pastoral work with the younger generations is in danger of having only a marginal impact. The reason is not hard to find: the key curriculum in the lives of young people is not school or church, or even home after a certain age, but culture and the zone of relationships. The fact that it is a hidden curriculum only increases its power and makes religious efforts to reach young people irrelevant unless they pay explicit attention to the surrounding cultural influences.

Against this background the history of youth ministry in recent decades is one of tension between different perspectives. In particular the period of the seventies saw three approaches in rivalry with one another, seeking to meet the changing cultural needs born in the sixties. One school was 'experiential' or existential, stressing the centrality of searching that started from young people themselves; unless evangelization paid attention to their felt needs and questions it would not prove fruitful. A second approach defended the continuing importance of 'content'; unless the teacher or preacher clarified the meaning of creed and church practices, the intellectual basis for faith would be absent. A third response highlighted 'community'; unless young people found opportunities for inter-personal sharing and belonging, they would never survive as believers amid the complex pressures of today.

All three tendencies had their own validity but all of them

remained somewhat innocent of the power of the emerging youth cultures. Of course these influences were not entirely negative. In spite of manipulation and superficiality, the youth cultures can be found to have their own sensibility to gospel values; much Church discourse can waste its energy in negativity – scapegoating the 'media' or 'pop music', for instance. Such generalized moaning belongs to the 'adversary' family of response described earlier, and lacks the precision of the real critique needed. The mass media may indeed be a source of triviality and apathy, and pop music can certainly be associated with mindless hedonism, but blanket condemnations cut little ice, particularly with young people. They can even feel it – from elders – as an insensitive dismissal of one of their natural environments and languages.

Within the last decade or so youth ministry has come to see the centrality of cultural discernment, but only as part of a larger convergence of responses. The three emphases just mentioned retain their importance but within a wider set of approaches – more developmental, more spiritual and more cultural.

'Developmental' includes all those insights into the slow process of possible Christian maturity: it draws on the wisdom of 'initiation' stages in the catechesis of the early centuries, and it sees young people in particular as being on a delicate journey of seeking and finding meaning for their lives. A gradualist understanding of youth ministry recognizes what growth points are ripe and what forms of faith are for the moment out of reach. Hence the inter-personal language that dominated some thinking in the seventies is now seen more as a necessary but incomplete stage of faith development. To foster only an inter-personal agenda could be a subtle form of stunted maturity, and one that will not last into adulthood. Indeed it is one of the temptations of contemporary culture to limit reality to the field of relationships, falling into what Richard Sennett terms 'the ideology of intimacy',[3] and avoiding tougher questions about social justice and about the larger forces at work in culture.

'Spirituality' has become, as already mentioned, a surprisingly central word in today's culture. It is evidence of a certain desperation for inner roots, or more positively, of a rediscovery of non-materialistic values – of silence and wonder, of qualities of heart-listening, of capacities for contemplative depth, ultimately a new hunger for genuine languages of personal prayer. Youth ministry has found that skills of stillness can be taught and that many young people can only arrive at some maturity of faith decision if they learn to listen to the Spirit in these quieter ways. But this dimension is not without its cultural deceptions: within youth culture narcissistic versions of 'New Age' spirituality can prove attractive, and result in a pseudo-spiritual cul-de-sac, meeting only those cultural tendencies to want transcendence on the cheap. Hence discernment of culture is particularly crucial, to protect the spiritual journey from mere self-exploration and to allow it to become a challenging encounter with the gospel.

Youth ministry has moved from the tensions between the schools of experience, content and community to include developmental and spiritual approaches, but 'cultural discernment' can be argued to be the most ambitious and difficult goal of youth ministry as understood today. As guides to this dimension of reflection on contemporary culture, I draw here on the works of Michael Warren and John Kavanaugh. Both authors focus on North American culture, Warren often from the point of view of communications and youth ministry, and Kavanaugh more from the perspective of a philosopher with a keen eye for social trends and the need for a spirituality of resistance today. Independently of one another, both have developed a style of aggressive discernment of culture. 'Aggressive' should not be interpreted as putting them into the camp of the 'tense adversaries'; it means rather that they argue forcefully against being too innocent about cultural control and oppression today. They both see such oppression as undermining, not so much Christian faith in itself, as the very possibility of believing, especially among the younger generations. To cite the phrase of St Paul once more, if 'faith comes from hearing', what in contemporary culture induces spiritual deafness? In this sense their work is a diagnosis of the causes of faith-deafness, not only in the general attitudes but in the lived 'practices' of our culture.

Warren's approach to culture is much influenced by Raymond Williams' insistence (examined in Chapter 1) that culture is not just a field of passive influences that happen to happen, but rather a signifying system for the 'production' of meaning. If culture involves patterns of interpreting reality, 'people do not so much believe in their society's patterns of thought and feeling; they approach life by means of them'.[4] In this way culture offers assumptions that become the unnoticed and pre-reflective paradigms people live by. Kavanaugh sees American culture as involving a clash between two sets of values, even though the battle zones are not always recognized. 'These competing life-forms can be expressed as the "gospels" of Personhood and Commodity.'[5] On the one hand there is the Christian vision of life as relationship or covenant between persons; on the other hand there is the idolatry of possessions, which undermines personhood and promotes a 'thing-ification' of existence, reducing even inter-personal areas of life to 'dominance and self-aggrandizement'.[6]

Behind these so-called 'habits of the heart' both authors see the pressures of politics and economics: the culture that shapes our hearts has identifiable roots in social forces that control our perceptions and, as in the case of advertising, do so with deliberate skill and foresight. One of Warren's key insights is that faith today cannot reach any healthy aliveness without awakening to the cultural curriculum that shapes people's attitudes into certain 'structures of feeling' (an expression from Williams). What is at stake here is an undermining of freedom for faith, and a resultant unreadiness for the gospel: against this imprisonment or unawareness 'coming to see that one has a way of seeing involves a shift in consciousness'.[7] Similarly for Kavanaugh a first step towards a Christian option of life entails realizing the pervasiveness of the commodity philosophy and the lived atheism that it assumes and promotes: only then can one come to recognize inevitable 'oppositions between cultural wisdom and Christian wisdom'.[8]

In an article with the indicative title 'The Material Conditions of Our Seeing and Perceiving', Warren highlights that the cultural space around us is far from neutral territory. It is full of messages that invite us to imitate various life-styles and that seek to shape our consciousness. If religious reflection forgets these factors, it will simply 'collude in enabling the conditions of our seeing to go unnoticed'.[9] But to become aware of the impact of social images is to begin to have a shield against deception and against the cultural coding that tries to manipulate attitudes.

Possibility of cultural agency

This awakening to a possible tyranny of images is only an initial stage in any cultural discernment. Warren and Kavanaugh are in agreement that some creative alternative is needed, in the form of Christian communities of lived resistance to the dominant culture. In this sense theoretical critique is not enough: more is needed than, for example, identifying the deceptions of consumerist values. Unless the Church moves towards being a producer of meaning, its discernment will remain passive. Faith-based communities must move towards 'cultural agency' because 'a religious culture of resistance is impossible unless it is grounded in patterned ways of living that embody an alternative vision of life'.[10] In today's cultural complexity it is self-defeating to think of evangelization as only a matter of communicating a 'message': it is also 'about the conditions of the practice of the Christian message'.[11]

Hence the living out of alternative visions within community is the only effective critique of the triviality fostered by the dominant culture. Warren likes to use the expression 'life structures' to point to a crucial area of cultural danger and of potential cultural resistance. It indicates an accumulation of daily choices, akin to what Rahner calls a 'fundamental option': it also suggests a pattern of habits and attitudes that do not easily change. The dominant culture pushes us towards egoist patterns; Christian faith aims at a radically different culture of self-transcendence and self-giving, which needs cultural incarnation as 'a gospel-based way of life in communities'.[12] To embody forms of Christian holiness for today's culture requires a special kind of community that avoids the trap of self-concern through 'individualized life-commitment, prayer, and the outreach to service'.[13]

The gospel saying that nobody can serve two masters finds its field of cultural conflict today on the level of human imagination, as a battle between different sets of symbols about what makes life worth living. And therefore a good way of alerting young people to this battle zone would be to ask them, 'Who is imaging your life for you?' Or else, 'Who is telling you stories that claim to show reality?' Christianity was always a story-telling and imagination-transforming vision. In many countries now children spend more time watching television than they spend in school; since most of them glean their images of the 'good life' from television, faith is faced not just with a secularizing force in the sitting room, but with a challenge to retell the Christian stories in ways that can rival the egoist myths. The idols of cultural imperialism need not only unmasking but rivalling and replacing.

In this respect Warren remains suspicious of various religious commentators on the mass media who look on them as a new instrument for communicating faith values; they can ignore the extent to which the media are totally 'embedded' in a commercially oriented world, a world expert in selling both products and attitudes through the bait of entertainment. This kind of culture is not genuinely 'of the people' but rather 'concocted for the consumption of the people'.[14] Media of this kind do not constitute a neutral instrument that needs only to be well used in order to produce good Christian fruit. If the roots of the tree are sick, the fruit cannot be untainted.

Do structures of sin inevitably underlie many expressions of popular culture? Even to pose such a question could seem to put one into the camp of the 'tense adversary', judgemental and dismissive of culture. But to shrug off the validity of the question puts one into the other extreme of the 'innocent accepter' who thinks everything is potentially good. How can we move beyond these inadequate stances towards seeing what Christian discernment entails? The example of television is a test case. Its more superficial productions unashamedly kidnap and colonize human attention with a fast-moving world of appearances. At its average worst television both fosters and assumes an uncritical passivity in its public. But in this respect it is a symbol and summary of all that is potentially dehumanizing in contemporary culture: it may only be the tip of the iceberg of false consciousness and of entrenched anti-culture. If so, some critical alertness will be a crucial first step towards cultural discernment, but Christian commitment calls for something more vigorous and creative.

Another Catholic voice that can not unfairly be classified as 'aggressive discernment' is that of the sociologist Kieran Flanagan. Against what he sees as the utopian optimism of Vatican II concerning culture and the dangerous innocence with which symbols of the sacred were later abandoned, he raises the question of the cultural 'construction and reproduction' of faith in today's world.[15] Insofar as the contemporary scene is dominated by a despiritualized ethos, more than a merely passive dialogue with the surrounding culture is required. It becomes a question of protecting the grounds for faith by educating 'sensibilities of belonging' by means of 'music, in skills of architecture, in styles of communal and ritual forms that seek to wrest the holy from the mundane'.[16] Like Warren and Kavanaugh, Flanagan highlights the counter-cultural formation of disposition and the crucial role of discernment:

> The problem theology faces is not of competing with the facile, but of securing fields of autonomy for the sacred, where expectations of discernment can be cultivated. These require the nurture of spiritual eyes to see and the cultivation of a disposition that wishes to notice the sacred.[17]

Towards creation of life structures

Cultural discernment has two phases, one of interpretation and judgement, and the other of communal spirituality and creation of Christian life structures. Together the two stages amount to that cultural agency whereby 'a person decides to exercise some judgment and control over the kinds of cultural material she/he will accept and the kinds that must be resisted'. Such agency will not only involve making reflective choices about 'the meanings and values created for us' in a given culture but active ways of 'examining and judging the *channels* by which these meanings and values are communicated to us'.[18] This means asking questions about power and about who benefits from the cultural situation as it is. We need a more penetrating level of inquiry than merely describing the cultural traits that happen to be dominant. They never just happen to be dominant, and this more aggressive discernment wants to know *why*.

If Warren and Kavanaugh are forceful in their negative critique of cultural oppressions and equally strong in their advocacy of cultural agency, they both seem hopeful about the potential of faith-rooted communities as sources of cultural discernment – on certain conditions. Church life in practice can fall into cowardly reproduction of the bias enthroned in the surrounding culture. But the prophetic call is to the opposite of such passive assimilation. We return to the idea that gives a title to this book: that a clash between cultures is inevitable, not always a clash of confrontation and total conflict, but a clash of two loyalties, an ambiguous set of influences to be sifted with spiritual wisdom. And such discernment is an essential gift of the religious imagination, because it seeks out the signs of love and self-giving that – in the Christian vision – are ultimately empowered by Christ but that are present as seeds in all that is good in human experience.

Particular tensions arise when Church institutions become servants or instruments of the wider culture. Instead of authentic inculturation, there is a real danger of what Kavanaugh calls 'acculturation' – in the sense of being absorbed in a compromising way into the dominant culture, thus losing its salt, as the gospel puts it. Without constant self-critique the Church can 'become too comfortable with Caesar' instead of subverting the domination of the 'commodity kingdom': 'If the Christian does feel at home, something is drastically wrong'.[19] An obvious example here is the Catholic school. Clearly the relation between the official faith-vision of the school and the unofficial cultural agenda lived in the daily praxis of both school and society will seldom be in a matter of 'sweetness and light' (as Arnold said in his humanistic view of culture). The Christian ideals of the institution may be subtly hijacked by the pressures of competition (from examinations to sport) or from the alternative curriculum of liberal relativism and self-fulfilment that is so easily absorbed from the wider culture. In this way youth ministry or religious schooling can fall into what Warren calls a 'Jesus reduction program', offering a soft picture of Christ that 'neatly fits the aspirations of middle-class' culture.[20]

However, if one points an accusing finger at the culture and its power to kidnap Church energies, in all justice one should equally put Church practices into the dock: the way the community acts can be a source of self-deception and of stunted conversion. Unless young people and lay people are given voice and power to participate in the formation of Church life, the Church itself is in danger of cultivating exactly the passivity that it might criticize in the

surrounding culture. It is not enough to be asked to foster 'reproduction of religious meaning'; each generation needs to forge an
'original production' of the Christian vision.[21] It is worth adding
that support for this line of thinking can be found, perhaps surprisingly, in Ludwig Wittgenstein's notebooks of reflections. There he
remarks that religious belief must be 'something like a passionate
commitment' that can only be taught in the 'form of a portrayal'.
Turning to the question of how to educate people towards faith, the
great philosopher writes: 'It would be as though someone were first
to let me see the hopelessness of my situation and then show me the
means of rescue until, of my own accord, or not at any rate led to it
by my *instructors*, I ran to it and grasped it'.[22]

Wittgenstein would start youth ministry (an expression he never
heard of!) with a diagnosis of need and follow up with a presentation of a way of life in full flow. Similarly this chapter has insisted
that the only fruitful answers to the seductive power of the culture
will come when Christian faith is lived together with creativity
and energy. There is a battle for people's minds and hearts and
imaginations. Individuals need the support of communities to forge
a Christian option that can survive. They also need a spirituality in
the wide sense of a whole way of life that nourishes Christian
commitment. But if a spirituality of cultural resistance is not simply
a matter of prayer alone, prayer nevertheless is a 'counter-cultural
act': 'it is a reappropriation of our personhood and identity'.[23]
Against the complexity of the cultural pressures today, only a convergence of Christian skills of resistance will bear fruit. To imagine
some of those possibilities will be the topic of the final chapter.

Chapter Twelve

Towards a Spirituality of Culture

> *Spirituality, the self's experience before God, occurs in history . . . in the forms and ways of seeing of a given culture.*
>
> (Veronica Brady)[1]

> *We live on one side of a great divide, where religion is something one thinks about rather than something one does.*
>
> (C. John Somerville)[2]

A poem by Seamus Heaney can offer an evocative opening for these final reflections. The title itself is significant: 'In Illo Tempore' ('at that time') used to be the opening words for the gospel reading in the Latin Mass. And the poem evokes an older world of saturating symbols and sacraments:

> The big missal splayed
> and dangled silky ribbons
> of emerald and purple and watery white.
>
> Intransitively we would assist,
> confess, receive.

A stanza later that communal 'we' changes to a lonely 'I' walking at night beside the sea:

> and even the range wall of the promenade
> that I press down on for conviction
> hardly tempts me to credit it.[3]

This captures something of the cultural-cum-religious change of these decades and the typical collapse of old securities, especially in Ireland. Only a generation ago, Catholicism meant largely that tighter universe or quasi-sacral community. We have since passed through a disturbing period of insecurity, but in recent years we may be reaching a new sensibility. Indeed in a recent interview

Seamus Heaney has remarked that our urge to secularize our lives was a mistake; he now insists more on the need to 'credit marvels' and to revisit thresholds of the spirit.

The transition from that anchored world of pre-modernity is seen from another angle in the second of the epigraphs above: in older times religion permeated culture, so much so that a religious culture seemed the only conceivable horizon of existence. When that habitual sense of the sacred disappears, either faith becomes a decision taken against the tide, or else it falls into that lostness imaged in Heaney's nocturnal walk on the beach. Granted these radical transformations, faith needs to forge new languages, starting with awareness of the culture, and going on to develop a capacity to 'think' and choose, to find the support of community, and most of all, to create a spirituality for living the gospel 'in' but not 'of' today's 'world'.

A recognition of the radically different culture that surrounds us today has been a constant theme in the various chapters of this book. It is also implied by the oft-repeated call by Pope John Paul II for a 'new evangelization', which he sees as responding to the new secular mood of culture, a situation requiring new depth and maturity of faith in people today. Hence evangelization has to be 'new in its urgency, in its methods, and in its expression'.[4]

Seamus Heaney's poem records an old world filled with sacramentality, but the enormous changes in culture have made that sensibility unreachable and unreal for many people today. Different roads need to be travelled towards the option of faith. What used to be a natural inheritance – a sense of the Christian sacred – has now to be built afresh, overcoming many desacralizing influences. And yet it is vital that reconstruction of faith be tackled not in a spirit of nostalgia or return to the past, nor in a spirit of hostility or resentment of the present. Since the call of God's Spirit is creative in the now of each culture, we need to read the situation with a trust that it too can become fertile ground for new languages of faith.

Meanings of spirituality today

The word 'spirituality', as used here, needs some initial comment, because its significance has changed hugely in recent years and it is in danger of becoming both vogue-ish and vague. Until the sixties, at least in Catholic circles, it was largely identified with the 'inner life', with individual prayer, and often with some tradition of a religious order (Benedictine, Jesuit, Carmelite, etc.). Now it has become a 'buzz-word' even outside Church circles (and sometimes to avoid the perceived narrowness of Church circles). It often suggests some school of self-ecology, a method of inner journeying, a counter-cultural option to cultivate awareness or self-development. As against the frequent association of old-style spirituality with asceticism (self-renunciation and the pursuit of perfection), contemporary spirituality prefers to be 'life-expanding' and incarnational, liberating a flow of divine energy in each person, and staying more in touch with the struggles of history.[5]

The older spiritualities were vertical roads of questing for God beyond this world. The newer ones stress a this-worldly fullness of life, as an experience of Christian faith. Influenced by the surrounding culture, with its hope for authenticity in the ordinary, do these more 'life-centred' approaches to spirituality reflect the 'eclipse of the transcendent'? Or, in their search for a more holistic living of faith, can this contemporary sensibility construct a new 'range of spirituality' different 'from any other time in human history'?[6]

The answer to that question lies at the heart of any Christian spirituality of culture. Of course not everyone would pose the question in those terms. Are we experiencing a cultural paradigm shift with lasting and revolutionary impact? Or are these upheavals in attitudes, and in Christianity itself, just passing tremors that will not change much in the long term? In some places the transformation is radical and represents a breakthrough into a new set of human assumptions. But where people are more rooted in tradition, the old languages seem to retain their validity. Any given parish or religious group is likely, on closer examination, to be surprisingly multicultural. Since, however, those older religious languages are no longer reaching those who move within the newer cultural worlds, it is clear that without a reimagined spirituality, Christianity is fated to become a museum piece for many in the younger generations. So this field is central for any evangelization of contemporary culture.

Sandra Schneiders offers an account of spirituality which remains open to Christian or secular interpretations: 'the experience of consciously striving to integrate one's life in terms not of isolation and self-absorption but of self-transcendence toward the ultimate value one perceives'.[7] Spirituality is a zone of convergence where theology, prayer and commitments come together as a 'conscious human response to God'.[8] It can also be approached psychologically in terms of an inner search for meaning, or more religiously as involving 'a process of conversion' of all aspects of one's life.[9]

In an explicitly Christian interpretation, spirituality seems to have three main thrusts today:

1.   It highlights the *lived experience* of faith, giving more attention to faith-response to God rather than to doctrine.

2.   It is *developmental* in the sense of fostering growth in contemplative and committed love.

3.   It teaches *practical* skills to nourish a conscious relationship with God through prayer and other reflective exercises.

Understood in this way, Christian spirituality has to do with building daily bridges between the gift of God in Christ and the limited realities of each one's life-situation. As such it is the essential link between faith and culture in most people's lives. It is the zone where they opt to give attention or not to the calls of the Spirit, where they shape the quality of their Christian journey, where they protect the freedom of their hearts, and where they learn to discern wisely amid the pressures of the culture. Adapting Socrates, the undiscerned and unlistening life is not worth living – especially so since we no longer live in premodernity and culture no longer carries us towards Christian faith. Either we drift confusedly in the culture around or we seize the rudder of spirituality to steer our course in harmony with the gospel.

Thus spirituality is a practical human art, for a more than human adventure. It starts from beyond us in God's desire to relate (amazingly) to us and to open the Trinity-Communion to us. In practice this means being led beyond ourselves into a slow erosion of egoism and a long learning of love. It entails a drama of receiving in order to give, one that echoes the story of Revelation itself. In this sense it is never simply the 'inner life': rather it is a whole way of wisdom where we grasp the gift of our freedom in Christ. And whenever that freedom and that gift are imperilled by the culture, spirituality can provide skills of self-defence.

The need for spiritual shields

Perhaps the greatest danger to our humanity within today's culture lies in being disconnected from our depths. Within each person is a whole cluster of capacities of the heart – for wonder, searching, listening, receptivity, and life options for compassion and love. These are spiritual dimensions in everyone and they constitute the basis for the hearing from which faith is born. But one by-product of the fragmentations and pressures of today is that this whole zone can remain underdeveloped. It is one form of cultural malnutrition (or cultural desolation, as discussed earlier). In the language of the parable of the Sower, culture can become a multi-faceted enemy for faith – robbing the seed, making shallow the roots, or choking the fragile plant.

When whole cultures remain 'trapped at the surface level', alienated from the deepest languages of our humanity, then 'reconnection with depth is the central issue'.[10] In older argumentation about faith one spoke about intellectual 'preambles' for belief in God. Now those preambles have to be spiritual, cultural and artistic, in order to prepare the receiving apparatus for faith by reopening contact points with human depth. We need rescuing from the surfaces where a certain kind of dominant culture can trap our spiritual sensibilities. How can this come about? Only through experiences that reach and liberate the imagination and the heart. Without 'preambles of disposition', to nourish wonder and invite into deeper levels of listening, the whole effort to make sense of God can be handicapped from the outset.[11] This is a task for poetry in the largest sense – not necessarily written poetry in verse, but various forms of imaginative communication that awaken the slumbering sense of mystery and of longing for something more. It is in this spirit that Vaclav Havel, while insisting on his own religious uncertainty, has quoted Heidegger's saying that 'only a God can save us now', and goes on to speak of today's multicultural world as needing to be 'rooted in self-transcendence'. Merely technological responses will not meet the hungers of our culture, because 'we are in a different place and facing a different situation' where the false confidence of modernity has to give way to 'something deeper'.[12]

The road of depth is certainly one of the avenues of hope for culture today, and for its religious renewal. But this emphasis on its own will not prove sufficient; indeed it can turn out to be a narcissistic turning inwards, a depth without contact with the calls of history or with the surprise of revelation. When 'uncoupled' from the cost and concreteness of the Bible, spirituality can serve merely 'therapeutic and self-expressive goals'.[13] In every age of culture, however, Christian faith has proved an extraordinary source of depth – through contemplative wisdom, or artistic creativity, or intellectual synthesis, or social vision. But this depth always saw itself as secondary to the gift of God in the Event of Christ. Christian interiority can never be content with mere withdrawal and serenity, because the cry of tragedy and injustice and the reminders of the prophets challenge that depth to do something about this wounded world, and to do so in God's name and in imitation of Christ. A renewal of depth is a crucial strand in the healing of our cultural impoverishments, but it is not the entire Christian response to culture.

Tensions in theology

It is not surprising to find that the tensions arising over the spirituality needed for contemporary culture find their parallels in theological polarities of today. Putting it very simply, there are at least three competing models of theology – liberation, dialogue and revelation. For the liberationist, faith has to shows itself in works, in praxis, in transformative commitment within the many justice battlegounds of history; otherwise it is in danger of being unfaithful to the prophetic call at the heart of the Bible and the contemporary cry of pain from the majority of people on our planet. Hence the approach to culture is one of critique, of aggressive discernment and of seeking to construct alternative communities of solidarity to counter the structural evils of today.

According to the dialogue model, we need to start from 'below', paying attention to the tone of human searching today. Theology needs to listen to the culture in its depth and even in its surfaces. Otherwise we risk unreality and irrelevance. To ignore the human hearer is insensitivity to the Incarnation. This stress on dialogue calls for contact in the first place but also for discernment, both positive and negative, trusting that we can discover signposts of the Spirit within contemporary hungers and questions.

For the revelation model, God has spoken 'from above', once and for all in Christ. All else is relative beside this Word as gift and judgement. Where the dialogue approach finds mediations of grace in the human, the revelationist stresses the disruptive beauty of God's wisdom and the fallacy of any anthropological yardsticks from the point of view of faith. All culture remains flawed and secondary because it is a human construct. Where the liberationist tends to interpret culture as structures in need of conversion, the revelationist views culture as the ground within which the seed has to be sown and a more transcendent Kingdom proclaimed. In brief, the liberation school offers a radical critique of culture as embodying assumptions of irresponsible escapism. The dialogue model prefers instead to listen for the deeper desires of the culture in its various levels. The revelation approach wants to recreate culture into Christian forms, to convert human attitudes to the unique light of the gospel.

In recent years, at least within Catholicism, there has been an unfortunate tendency to ideologize and polarize these stances. It is strange to run into those who will read and follow only von Balthasar or only Rahner or only Gutiérrez, and see the positions of others as almost heretical. However, if we shift the wavelength from ideas to spirituality, what seem like incompatible divergences can be found to converge into a potentially important unity. There are undoubtedly major divergences between these theologians; confronted, however, with the acute pastoral crisis of our culture, they discover a new harmony, where each emphasis is essential for modelling an alternative Christian culture to rival the dominant imagination.

In a recent book, James Bacik speaks of a 'postmodern spirituality which is more attuned to the mystery dimension of life', and he lists some of its possible characteristics.[14] As against the individualistic and rationalist approaches fostered by modernity, the postmodern moment calls forth different tones: 'more communal, intuitive and reflective'; 'explicitly relational'; pluralistic, combining 'acceptance and protest', as well as the mystical and the prophetic dimensions of faith. Independently I had prepared the following diagram that echoes much the same line of thought. It is intended to show – in a deliberately simplified form – how some principal features of the postmodern sensibility awaken ancient dimensions of Christian faith, so that they find new energy and relevance within the culture of today.

Postmodern sensibility	*Notes within faith*
1. Distrust of rationalism	Narrative and negative theology
2. Awareness of the feminine and the ecological	Christian connectedness/ holism
3. Quest for post-materialist quality of life	Gospel as an alternative 'Way'
4. Return of spirituality	Contemplative skills of prayer
5. Sense of dispersal	Community as support
6. Disillusion with utopias	Compassion and social solidarity

1.   Down through the ages faith has always had to insist that while it is reasonable, it goes beyond the merely rationalist because it depends on God's revelation; theology today is recovering an appreciation of its roots in story and in beauty, as well as a sense of its darkness as a mystery beyond the excessive clarity of words and concepts.

2.   From its understanding of Creation and Incarnation, Christian faith has a special reverence for the material world and for humanity as its crown. Those aspects of spirituality were somewhat neglected in recent centuries but are now re-emerging under the impetus of secular developments; faith can find inspiration from cultural sensibilities born outside the Church (as acknowledged in *Gaudium et Spes*, No. 44).

3.   Faith always meant a conversion of heart through accepting the gospel; today, faced with the often shallow way of life promoted by

the dominant culture, we realize more dramatically that Christian faith is a radically different 'Way' (that word being one of the New Testament terms for living out one's yes to Christ).

The final three constitute the essential pillars of faith in every age: from the Acts of the Apostles onwards Christianity fostered (4) worship, (5) belonging and (6) active service of those in need. Similarly, Christian spirituality for today's culture needs a triple initiation – of contemplative depth, of experience of community, and of lived options of self-giving.

4.   Ronald Rolheiser speaks of the emergence in today's culture of a new 'non-contemplative personality' with a shrunken capacity for wonder and for inner awareness.[15] Where people learn to pray personally they are escaping from that narrow prison of utilitarian living, precisely through encountering what is at the heart of the revelationist's concern: the uniqueness of Christ.

5.   Where they discover the slow journey of dialogue with others, and when they learn through that companionship and searching, they come in contact with the human tone of today's culture in a way that would satisfy the dialogue model.

6.   Whenever they learn through contact with the pain of others that they have a generosity within them that the world needs, and if they choose to commit themselves in some concrete road of service or struggle, then they are in touch with what liberation spirituality calls conversion through praxis.

A convergence to meet a convergence

Martin Buber once commented that the real danger of Egypt was that the Israelites would come to think of the situation there as normal. Our temptation is to think of the culture that kidnaps the imagination, rendering faith unreachable for many, as somehow beyond question: it's the way things are. But there are wiser responses to the omnipresent and omni-shaping culture than a shrug of the shoulders or merely a turning of the back, a locking of Christian doors in defensiveness. This book has suggested analysis, discernment, critique and cultural creation as essential notes in the chord of faith today. Throughout these pages it has been seen how complex a presence culture is, how it involves a convergence of influences that reach us all on the level of the imagination. Not all those influences are malign but many are trivializing, confusing or ambiguous. Only a Christian convergence of strengths can counter this convergence of cultural impoverishments. And the Christian answer has to meet its opponent on the level of experience, imagination and spirituality.

But ambiguities abound. That simple realization is forced on us again as we come to the end of this book. Paul Tillich, a pioneer in the field of theology of culture, spoke of a 'spiritual community' which in theory would be 'unambiguous', a perfect situation where 'culture is the form of religion and religion the substance of culture'. That unity, however, does not exist; we live rather with the 'existential separation' of faith and culture, where the churches seek to be cultural mediations of the gospel but, alas, often constitute cultural distortions of faith.[16] Faced with all these tensions and ambiguities, some of the older religious optimism about culture can seem naive. In practice much of the unbelief of today is 'less due to secularisation than to a failure to discern contemporary culture and to find a means of connecting to it'.[17] The more one reflects on this whole field of faith-and-culture, the more it reveals its importance but also its complications.

How can a balance be found between excessive fear and excessive innocence? In an interview towards the end of his life, Hans Urs von Balthasar commented that there should be no distrust of modern culture on the part of Christians, *provided* 'adequate spiritual discernment is exercised'.[18] In spite of some destructive aspects of contemporary life-styles that can have a 'seductive influence' on young people, he went on to insist that faith seek to create culture, and that Christians should commit themselves 'to the whole of secular culture', building 'islands of humanity' in order to 'humanize whatever is threatening to slide into the inhuman'.[19]

To repeat and conclude: there are three converging strengths to be learned – skills of interiority, supports of community, and commitment to service of the wounded of the world. They constitute a pastoral triangle as old as the Acts of the Apostles but as fresh as any alert Christian community today. Where any one of these growth languages is alive and well, there is hope for faith in spite of the complexity of the culture. Where all three flourish, we are well on the way to recreating a living Christian culture for our time.

A Personal Epilogue

Roots and Horizons

> *You must wait for the eye of the soul to be formed in you. Religious truth is reached, not by reasoning, but by an inward perception.*
>
> (John Henry Newman)[1]

> *Everybody knows that we make sense of the past by telling stories. I suspect we make sense of the future by telling those stories as well.*
>
> (Robert Wuthnow)[2]

I had not planned to write this section but I want to end with something simpler and more personal. This book has been complex and theoretical at times. So, what does it all mean for me? What is my 'culture'? Has it changed with the years? What cultures have formed me? How is it different for the new generation? Answering those questions fully might require an autobiography. But some random reflections may serve as a conclusion and invite the reader to ponder her or his story of this strange reality called culture.

Recently I revisited the village of my childhood – Collooney, Co. Sligo, in the north-west of Ireland. I was touring with Italian friends and they were interested in seeing where I had grown up. With them I went into the 'sitting room' of the house where I spent my first fifteen years and bought a bar of chocolate! That part of the house is now a shop. The owners were strangers to me; in fact I have no relations in the village any more. Later we met people that I knew, who gave me a warm welcome 'home'; but I realized that only a certain age group had any idea of who I was. With the Italians I walked down the one main street of the village, where I could remember every house and who lived there in the forties and fifties. We went into the church were I had been an altar server for years. Everything seemed vivid like yesterday except that yesterday seemed another world.

This village *was* my culture. 'We were as Danes in Denmark all day long': a line from Wallace Stevens sums it up – a small and total world, which moulded how I feel and imagine everything, even today. Or to quote Yeats (himself from Sligo) a certain 'unity of culture' was strong in my formative years. Since then I have had to learn to move in more complex worlds. Even the fact of walking through Collooney speaking Italian symbolized how horizons had changed. In the small schoolroom, with its turf fire that the rain used to put out, we had studied the geography of Europe (in Gaelic). Now I have been to places I never noticed on the rotating globe on the windowsill: India, Venezuela, Paraguay, Ethiopia, Australia, New Zealand, Japan, Iran, Malaysia. That village and that family sitting room shaped my roots – and they remain steady – but it is no longer my horizon of culture. On the spot where we listened to the old 'wireless' a cash register now stands. The school itself is a shed for cattle.

Let me switch scene. I have been living in Rome for nearly six years now. Sometimes as I walk to the university, to teach theology, I watch the faces in the streets. Since I am on my way to some class about faith, I find myself wondering about the religious roots, or lack of them, in the young people around me. I become aware of a whole range of nourishment – of the spirit and the imagination – that my childhood gave me; but these young Romans have had little opportunity of this kind. I imagine them lonely in surprising ways: where do they have real community beyond the small circles of friendship? I sense them drifting on the surface of themselves: where do they have languages of wonder that might open towards God? I feel that they have much to give but few channels for giving. They seem more like victims of this moment in history than lost in laziness or egoism. I picture them, spiritually, as uncalled, unawoken, unreached by the Truth that for me is at the centre of life. What is missing? That unity of culture that Collooney gave me, except that for them it would have to be chosen and created – because their more broken context leaves them (and me, in ways) more stranded from reality, from our true humanity, from God. Are my Roman musings too pessimistic? A bit like St Paul in his first reaction to Athens? If so, I need to wait, like him, until I can glimpse the signs of searching beyond the appearances.

Certainly the village world is gone. Mourning its passing is waste of time. The cities that we 'bought' into (and the word is right) have given us exciting freedoms but many confusions. The contrast with my childhood seems clear. Without idealizing or exaggerating (I hope), that village world gave me roots that have been a constant, if often unconscious, blessing. They have been like an anchor that allowed leeway for movement, freedom for change, for other languages in every sense. Where will the children of the city find anchors and roots? In family experience which is the core stability in spite of cultural change?[3] In encountering the stories and symbols of God through the Church? What experiences and images could liberate their hope and incarnate the gospel for them?

Broadening the picture, is our whole culture in flight, not just from roots, from the cost of love? The recurring tragedies of war or famine, together with the stagnant situations of injustice, show that something is sick in how we live and in how we manage this planet. We seem to remain paralysed behind the walls our cultural egoism has constructed. Impotence of imagination rules. Distortions come to seem normal. In the light of faith the conclusion is unoriginal but clear: Christianity has to enter this battle zone of clashing symbols, in the spirit of a servant, so that redemptive love can undermine the 'imperial' images of a closed culture.[4] Bernard Lonergan once wondered whether a culture can recover from decline: 'To my mind the only solution is religious . . . when reasoning is ineffective, what is left but faith', the faith that has as its core an image of 'self-sacrificing love'?[5] Thus the healing of our ills lies in discovering love through God, or God through love – two different journeys that converge to give a special tone to being a Christian in today's culture.

Let me close with another recent experience: together with some relations I visited the National Gallery in Dublin. We were a group of three adults and five children (aged seven to thirteen). The problem of how not to bore the children solved itself in the best postmodern way! We left them in the new computer section of the Gallery, where they happily explored the world of art, fingering the screens of monitors and listening on earphones – allowing the adults to see the real paintings in peace. On our return the children hardly wanted to leave the computers; it was marvellous to watch their ease with technology (I who am slowly learning the secrets of

Windows 95 and have not yet surfed into the Net). But will their roots be radically different from ours? Will they ever want to see the real pictures? Are we on the threshold of a major cultural shift?

I do not know. But thinking now of the contrast between my childhood and that of the young today, culture seems like a dialogue between roots and horizons. The roots come early in life; the novelist Mauriac claimed that the doors of imagination close at twenty. But then comes the longer adventure of changing horizons. Perhaps faith can best flourish and 'become culture' by entering that dialogue – connecting roots of sensibility and the courage of change, and by echoing *the* image of love that liberates both hearts and cultures.

Anthology of Quotations on Culture

The extracts are in chronological order.

It is one of the marks of the human person to reach true and authentic humanity only through culture, that is, by cultivating natural gifts and values. Whenever human life is involved, nature and culture are intimately connected.

In its general sense the word 'culture' stands for everything by which human beings refine and develop their various capacities of mind and body. It includes efforts to control the cosmos by knowledge or by work, as well as ways of humanizing social life within the family or civic community through the progress of customs and institutions.

(Second Vatican Council, *Gaudium et Spes*, 1965, no. 53)

A theology mediates between a cultural matrix and the significance and role of a religion in that matrix. The classicist notion of culture was normative: at least *de jure* there was but one culture that was both universal and permanent; to its norms and ideals might aspire the uncultured, whether they were the young or the people or the natives or the barbarians. Besides the classicist, there also is the empirical notion of culture. It is the set of meanings and values that informs a way of life. It may remain unchanged for ages. It may be in process of slow development or rapid dissolution.

(Bernard Lonergan, *Method in Theology,* Darton, Longman & Todd, London, 1972, p. xi)

The Church is an evangelizer, but it begins by being evangelized itself . . . if it wants to retain freshness, vigour, and strength in order to proclaim the Gospel . . .

What matters is to evangelize human culture and cultures (not in a purely decorative way as it were by applying a thin veneer, but in a vital way, in depth and right to their very roots) . . . always taking the person as one's starting point and always coming back to the relationship of people among themselves and with God.

The Gospel, and therefore evangelization, are certainly not identical with culture, and they are independent in regard to all cultures. Nevertheless, the Kingdom which the Gospel proclaims is lived by people who are profoundly linked to a culture, and the building up of the Kingdom cannot avoid borrowing the elements of human culture or cultures. Though independent of cultures, the Gospel and evangelization are not necessarily incompatible with them; rather they are capable of permeating them all without becoming subject to any one of them.

The split between the Gospel and culture is without doubt the drama of our time, just as it was of other times. Therefore every effort must be made to ensure a full evangelization of culture, or more correctly of cultures.

(Paul VI, *Evangelii nuntiandi*, 1975, §§ 15, 20)

[Culture] means simply the patterned way in which people do things together . . . Culture implies a measure of homogeneity . . . Culture holds people together over a span of time. It is received from the past, but not by any process of natural inheritance. It has to be learned afresh by each generation . . . Culture covers everything in human life. At its centre is a world-view, that is, a general understanding of the nature of the universe and of one's place in it . . . From this basic world-view flow both standards of judgement or values and standards of conduct . . . Cultures are never static; there is a continuous process of change . . .

[In synthesis] Culture is an integrated system of beliefs (about God or reality or ultimate meaning), of values (about what is true, good, beautiful and normative), of customs (how to behave, relate to others, talk, pray, dress, work, play, trade, farm, eat, etc.) and of institutions which express those beliefs, values and customs . . . which bind a society together and gives it a sense of identity, dignity, security, and continuity.

(From the Willowbank Report, Lausanne Committee for World Evangelization, 1978)

I stress the necessity of mobilizing all sources which direct the spiritual dimension of human existence, and which bear witness to the primacy of the spiritual in humanity – and which corresponds to the dignity of intelligence, will and heart – in order not to succumb again to the monstrous alienation of collective evil . . . (4)

Thanks to culture a person lives a really human life. Human life is culture in this sense too that, through it, human beings are distinguished and differentiated from everything that exists in the visible world: human beings cannot do without culture . . . In the unity of culture as the specific way of human existence, there is rooted at the same time the plurality of cultures within which people live. In this plurality, a person develops without losing, however, the essential contact with the unity of culture as the fundamental and essential dimension of one's existence and being. (6)

The human being who, in the visible world, in the only ontic subject of culture, is also its only object and its term. Culture is that through which the human being, as human, becomes more human, 'is' more, has more access to 'being' . . . People think of culture and speak about it in the first place in relation to the nature of the human being, then only in a secondary and indirect way in relation to the world of human products . . . A human being, and only a human being, is the 'protagonist' or 'architect' of culture . . . (7)

Human cultures reflect, there is no doubt, the various systems of production relations; however, it is not such and such a system that is at the origin of culture, but human beings, who live in the system, who accept it or try to change it. A culture without human subjectivity and without human causality is inconceivable; in the cultural field, the human being is always the first fact – the prime and fundamental fact of culture. And one is so, always, in one's totality: in one's spiritual and material subjectivity as a complete whole . . . (8)

[There exists a] fundamental link between the Gospel, that is, the message of Christ and the Church, and a human being in one's very humanity. This link is in fact a creator of culture in its very foundation. To create culture, it is necessary to consider, to its last consequences and entirely, the human being as a particular and autonomous value, as the subject bearing the transcendency of the person. Human beings must be affirmed for themselves, and not for any other motive or reason: solely for themselves! (10)

The future of humanity depends on culture. (23)

(John Paul II, UNESCO, Paris, 2 June 1980)

Culture may now be said to be the whole complex of distinctive features, spiritual, material, intellectual and emotional, that characterize a society or social group. It includes not only the arts and letters, but also modes of life, the fundamental rights of human being, value systems, traditions and beliefs ... It is culture that gives the ability to reflect. It is culture that makes us specifically human, rational beings, endowed with critical judgement and a sense of moral commitment. It is through culture that we discern values and make choices. It is through culture that human beings express themselves, become aware of themselves, recognize their incompleteness, question their own achievements, seek untiringly for new meanings and create works through which they transcend their limitations.

(UNESCO definition, Mexico conference, 1982)

Culture is the expression of the identity of a human community. Culture refers to the delicate fabric of habits, symbols, artistic representations, tools, rules of behaviour, moral values and institutions through which the human community orders its relationships to nature, to other communities and to reality as a whole. Through processes of socialisation and through tradition, a culture is being transmitted to the following generations. In this sense, culture is specifically human; it is the second 'nature' of human beings in their social relationships. Any understanding of culture includes the language, history, family patterns, etc. of a given community.

(Konrad Raiser, Secretary General, WCC, 1994)

Notes

Introduction

1. T. S. Eliot, *Notes towards the Definition of Culture* (Faber & Faber, London, 1948), p. 27.
2. Robert M. Doran, *Theology and the Dialectics of History* (University of Toronto Press, Toronto, 1990), p. 548.
3. Samuel Huntington, 'The Clash of Civilizations?', *Foreign Affairs*, Summer 1993, pp. 22–49. Quotations from pp. 22, 31.
4. Anthony D. Smith, *National Identity* (Penguin Books, London, 1991), pp. 155, 159.
5. Fred Inglis, *Cultural Studies* (Blackwell, Oxford, 1993), pp. xi, 247.
6. Stephen L. Carter, *The Culture of Disbelief: how American Law and Politics Trivialize Religious Devotion* (Basic Books, New York, 1993), pp. 22, 25, 44.
7. Bernard Lonergan, *Method in Theology* (Darton, Longman & Todd, London, 1972), p. xi.
8. Bernard Lonergan, *Collection*, ed. F. E. Crowe (Darton, Longman & Todd, London, 1967), p. 266.
9. Aylward Shorter, *Towards a theology of inculturation* (Geoffrey Chapman, London, 1988), p. 4.
10. This phrase is from Raymond Williams, *The Long Revolution* (Chatto & Windus, London, 1961), p. 48.
11. Edward T. Hall, *Beyond Culture* (Anchor Books, New York, 1977), p. 85.

Chapter 1

1. Margaret Miles, *Image as Insight: Visual Understanding in Western Christianity and Secular Culture* (Beacon Press, Boston, 1985), p. 3.
2. Avery Dulles, an unpublished lecture of 13 May 1996 on '*Centesimus annus* and the Renewal of Culture'. Text kindly given to me by the author.
3. Matthew Arnold, *Culture and Anarchy*, ed. R. H. Super (University of Michigan Press, Ann Arbor, 1965), pp. 95, 112.
4. Edward B. Tylor, *Primitive Culture* (John Murray, London, 1871), Vol. I, p. 1.
5. Quoted in Lawrence Osborn, *Restoring the Vision: The Gospel and Modern Culture* (Mowbray, London, 1995), p. 1.

6. A. L. Kroeber and Clyde Kluckhohn, *Culture: A Critical Review of Concepts and Definitions* (Vintage Books, New York, 1963).

7. *ibid.*, p. 128.

8. Clifford Geertz, *The Interpretation of Cultures* (Basic Books, New York, 1973), p. 89.

9. *ibid.*, p. 5.

10. Robert J. Schreiter, *Constructing Local Theologies* (SCM Press, London, 1985), p. 55.

11. Geertz, *op.cit.*, pp. 17, 28.

12. *ibid.*, p. 44.

13. *ibid.*, p. 46.

14. Clifford Geertz, *Local Knowledge: Further Essays in Interpretive Anthropology* (Basic Books, New York, 1983), p. 85.

15. *Local Knowledge*, p. 75.

16. Bernard Lonergan, *Insight: a study of human understanding* (Longman Green, London, 1958), pp. 179, 419, 237.

17. *Insight*, p. 236.

18. Bernard Lonergan, *Method in Theology* (Darton, Longman & Todd, London, 1972), p. 301.

19. Bernard Lonergan, *A Second Collection*, ed. W. Ryan and B. Tyrrell (Darton, Longman & Todd, London, 1974), p. 101.

20. Raymond Williams, *The Long Revolution* (Chatto & Windus, London, 1961), p. 41.

21. *ibid.*, pp. 48, 72.

22. Raymond Williams, *Culture and Society* (Hogarth Press, London, 1993), 1958 Introduction, p. xvi.

23. Raymond Williams, 'Culture is Ordinary', reprinted in *Studying Culture: an introductory reader*, ed. Ann Gray and Jim McGuigan (Edward Arnold, London, 1993), pp. 5–14. Quotation from p. 6.

24. Raymond Williams, *Culture* (Fontana, London, 1981). pp. 10–12.

25. *Culture and Society*, p. 325.

26. *Culture*, p. 209.

27. *ibid.*, p. 13.

28. *ibid.*, p. 206.

29. Pierre Bourdieu et al., *Academic Discourse* (Polity Press, Cambridge, 1994), p. 8; Bourdieu, *Algeria 1960: The Disenchantment of the World* (Cambridge, Cambridge University Press, 1979), p. vii.

30. As quoted by Hervé Carrier, in *The Church and Culture since Vatican II*, ed. Joseph Gremillion (University of Notre Dame Press, Notre Dame, 1985), p. 19.

31. See Charles R. Taber, *The world is too much with us: 'culture' in modern Protestant missions* (Mercer University Press, Macon, 1991), p. 5.

Chapter 2

1. Mary Douglas, 'The Effects of Modernization on Religious Change', in *Religion and America: Spiritual Life in a Secular Age*, ed. M. Douglas and S. Tipton (Beacon Press, Boston, 1983), p. 26.
2. Walter J. Ong, *Frontiers in American Catholicism* (Macmillan, New York, 1961), p. 102.
3. Mary Douglas, *Natural Symbols: Explorations in Cosmology* (Cresset Press, London, 1970), p. x.
4. *ibid.*, p. ix.
5. Mary Douglas, *In the Wilderness* (Academic Press, Sheffield, 1993), p. 47.
6. Mary Douglas, *Risk and Blame: essays in cultural theory* (Routledge, London, 1992), p. 125.
7. See Gerald A. Arbuckle, *Refounding the Church* (Geoffrey Chapman, London, 1993), p. 81.
8. *Natural Symbols*, p. 60.
9. *In the Wilderness*, pp. 45, 47.
10. *ibid.*, p. 4.
11. Arbuckle, *op. cit.* p. 88.
12. *In the Wilderness*, p. 44.
13. *Risk and Blame*, pp. 136–7.
14. Margaret Archer, *Culture and Agency: the place of culture in social theory* (Cambridge University Press, Cambridge, 1988), pp. xv, xxii.
15. *ibid.*, pp. 12, 18.
16. *ibid.*, pp. 293, 289.
17. *ibid.*, p. xv.
18. Walter Ong, *Orality and Literacy: the Technologizing of the Word* (Routledge, London, 1982), pp. 78, 178–9.
19. Walter J. Ong, *The Presence of the Word: Some Prolegomena for Culture and Religious History* (Simon & Schuster, New York, 1970), pp. 111, 117.
20. *Presence of the Word*, p. 125. See also Ong, *Ramus, Method, and the Decay of Dialogue* (Harvard University Press, Cambridge, 1958).
21. Walter J. Ong, *Interfaces of the Word: Studies in the Evolution of Consciousness and Culture* (Cornell University Press, Ithaca, 1977), p. 222.
22. Walter J. Ong, *Faith and Contexts* [Collected Essays 1952–1991], 2 vols, ed. Thomas Farrell (Scholars Press, Atlanta, 1992), II, 162.

Chapter 3

1. Quoted by Frederick Crowe in *Bernard Lonergan* (Geoffrey Chapman, London, 1992), p. 98.

2. Dermot Lane, ed., *Religion and Culture in Dialogue* (Columba Press, Dublin, 1993), p. 14.

Chapter 4

1. Margaret O'Brien Steinfels, 'Beyond Assimilation: Let's get wise', in *The Catholic Church and American Culture*, ed. Cassian Yuhaus (Paulist Press, New York, 1990), p. 36.
2. Michael Novak, *The Catholic Ethic and the Spirit of Capitalism* (Free Press, New York, 1993), p. 214.
3. Fernando Miguens, *Fe y Cultura en la Enseñanza de Juan Pablo II* (Ediciones Palabra, Madrid, 1994).
4. Avery Dulles, 'The Prophetic Humanism of John Paul II', *America* (23 October 1993), p. 9.
5. Miguens, *op. cit.*, pp. 169–70 (my translation).

Chapter 5

1. Quoted in S. Wesley Ariarajah, *Gospel and Culture: An Ongoing Discussion within the Ecumenical Movement* (Gospel and Cultures Pamphlet 1, WCC Publications, Geneva, 1994), p. 28.
2. 'On Intercultural Hermeneutics' [Report of a WCC theological consultation, Jerusalem, December 1995], *International Review of Mission* (Vol. 85, No. 337, 1996), p. 242.
3. Konrad Raiser, 'Gospel and Cultures', *International Review of Mission* (Vol. 83, No. 331, 1994), p. 623.
4. Emilio Castro, 'On Evangelism and Culture: Some Reflections', *International Review of Mission* (Vol. 84, No. 335, pp. 365–78). References here are to pp. 366–7.
5. S. Wesley Ariarajah, *op. cit.* In the following paragraphs, which summarize this fine essay, page references will be given in parenthesis in the text.
6. *Study Process on Gospel and Cultures* (WCC, Geneva, 1995), p. 6.
7. Christopher Duraisingh, 'Looking towards Salvador: editorial', *International Review of Mission* (Vol. 84, No. 334, 1995), p. 206.
8. These questions are paraphrased from pp. 6–18 of the Study Process booklet mentioned in Note 6.
9. Christopher Duraisingh, 'Authentic Witness Within Each Culture: Editorial', *International Review of Mission* (Vol. 84, No. 335, 1995), pp. 361–2.

Chapter 6

1. Charles Baudelaire, *The Painter of Modern Life* (Phaidon Press, Oxford, 1964), p. 3.
2. Jane Collier in *The Gospel and Contemporary Culture*, ed. Hugh Montefiore (Mowbray, London, 1992), p. 112.
3. Stuart Hall, 'The Question of Cultural Identity', in *The Polity Reader in Cultural Theory* (Polity Press, Cambridge, 1994), p. 119.
4. Kieran Flanagan, *Sociology and Liturgy: Re-presentations of the Holy* (Macmillan, London, 1991), p. 324.
5. Leszek Kolakowski, *Modernity on Endless Trial* (University of Chicago Press, Chicago, 1990), p. 6.
6. Louis Dupré, *Passage to Modernity* (Yale University Press, New Haven, 1993), *passim*.
7. Hannah Arendt, *The Human Condition* (University of Chicago Press, Chicago, 1958), p. 248.
8. *ibid.*, p. 305.
9. Dupré, *op. cit.*, p. 249.
10. *Autonomy and Solidarity: Interviews with Jürgen Habermas*, ed. Peter Dews (Verso, London, 1992), pp. 225, 227.
11. Alain Touraine, *Critique of Modernity* (Blackwell, Oxford, 1995), p. 340.
12. *ibid.*, pp. 345, 29.
13. *ibid.*, p. 314.
14. *ibid.*, p. 292.
15. *ibid.*, pp. 322, 318.
16. Charles Taylor, *Sources of the Self: the making of modern identity* (Harvard University Press, Cambridge, 1989), p. 429.
17. *ibid.*, pp. 506–507, p. 520.
18. Charles Taylor, *The Ethics of Authenticity* (Harvard University Press, Cambridge, 1991), p. 10.
19. *ibid.*, pp. 17–18.
20. *ibid.*, p. 16.
21. *ibid.*, p. 35.
22. *ibid.*, p. 69.
23. *ibid.*, pp. 118, 101.

Chapter 7

1. Walter Benjamin, *Charles Baudelaire* (New Left Books, London, 1973), p. 151.
2. José Casanova, *Public Religions in the modern world* (University of Chicago Press, Chicago, 1994), p. 234.
3. *L'Osservatore Romano*, 25 September 1994, p. 5.
4. Casanova, *op. cit.*, pp. 214, 234.

5. See Gilles Langevin, 'L'inculturation selon le magistère de l'Eglise catholique romaine', *Nouveau Dialogue* (Montreal, No. 97, 1993), p. 23.

6. Christopher Dawson, *Religion and Culture* (Sheed & Ward, London, 1948), p. 217.

7. Christopher Dawson, *Understanding Europe* (Sheed & Ward, London, 1952), pp. 241, 244–5.

8. Romano Guardini, *The End of the Modern World* (Sheed & Ward, London, 1957), pp. 52, 56.

9. *ibid.*, p. 61.

10. *ibid.*, pp. 97–8.

11. Romano Guardini, *Letters from Lake Como* (Ressourcement edition, William Eerdmans, Grand Rapids, 1994), pp. 63, 80, 81.

12. *The End of the Modern World*, pp. 112–113.

13. Hervé Carrier, *Evangelizing the Culture of Modernity* (Orbis Books, New York, 1993), p. 35.

14. *ibid.*, p. 42.

15. *ibid.*, p. 62.

16. Lesslie Newbegin, *Gospel in a Pluralist Society* (SPCK, London, 1989), pp. 187–9.

17. Newbegin, *Foolishness to the Greeks* (SPCK, London, 1986), p. 24.

18. *ibid.*, p. 58.

19. Lesslie Newbegin, 'Ecumenical Amnesia', *International Bulletin of Missionary Research* (Vol. 18, January 1994), pp. 2–5. Quotations from p. 3.

20. Its current director is Dr Andrew Walker and it has offices in the theological department of King's College London.

21. Lawrence Osborn, *Restoring the Vision: the Gospel and Modern Culture* (Mowbray, London, 1995), p. 146.

22. *ibid.*, pp. 76, 147.

23. *The Gospel and Contemporary Culture*, ed. Hugh Montefiore (Mowbray, London, 1992). Quotation from Montefiore's introduction, pp. 4–5.

24. *Catholicism and Secularization in America: Essays on Nature, Grace, and Culture*, ed. David L. Schindler (Communio Books, Notre Dame, 1990). Quotation from p. 12 of Schindler's introduction.

25. *ibid.*, pp. 19–20.

26. David Schindler, 'Christological aesthetics and *Evangelium Vitae*: Towards a definition of liberalism', *Communio* (Vol. 22, 1995), pp. 198–9.

27. *ibid.*, pp. 215, 217.

28. David Schindler, 'Faith and the Logic of Intelligence: Secularization and the Academy', *op. cit.* (1990), p. 175.

29. *art. cit.* (1995), pp. 223–4.

30. *art. cit.* (1995), p. 200.

31. See David Tracy, 'The Uneasy Alliance Reconceived: Catholic theo-

logical method, modernity, and postmodernity', *Theological Studies* (Vol. 50, 1989), 548–70.

Chapter 8

1. Mary Midgley in *The Gospel and Contemporary Culture*, ed. Hugh Montefiore (Mowbray, London, 1992), p. 53. Parts of this chapter have appeared in *Faith and Culture in the Irish Context*, ed. Eoin G. Cassidy (Veritas Publications, Dublin, 1996).

2. Zygmunt Bauman, *Intimations of Postmodernity* (Routledge, London, 1992), p. x.

3. Anthony Giddens, *The Consequences of Modernity* (Polity Press, Cambridge, 1990), p. 3.

4. See Michael J. Buckley, *At the Origins of Modern Atheism* (Yale University Press, New Haven, 1987).

5. See Charles Taylor, *Sources of the Self: the making of modern identity* (Harvard University Press, Cambridge, 1989).

6. Charles Taylor, *The Ethics of Authenticity* (Harvard University Press, Cambridge, 1991), p. 120.

7. David Tracy, 'Theology and the Many Faces of Postmodernity', *Theology Today* (Vol. 51, 1994), pp. 104–114. Quotations from pp. 104–107.

8. See José María Mardones, *El desafío de la postmodernidad al cristianismo* (Sal Terrae, Santander, 1988); Luis González-Carvajal, *Ideas y creencias del hombre actual* (Sal Terrae, Santander, 1991); Alejandro Llano, *La nuova sensibilità: il positivo della società postmoderna*, (Ares, Milan, 1995).

9. Elizabeth Johnson, 'Between the Times: religious life and the postmodern experience of God', *Review for Religious* (Vol. 53, 1994), pp. 6–28. Quotations from pp. 18–19.

10. Elaine L. Graham, *Transforming Practice: Pastoral Theology in an Age of Uncertainty* (Mowbray, London, 1996), pp. 18, 206.

11. George Steiner, *Real Presences* (Faber, London, 1989), pp. 3, 228.

12. David Walsh, *After Ideology: Recovering the Spiritual Foundations of Freedom* (Catholic University of America Press, Washington, DC, 1990), pp. 1–2.

13. John Haldane, 'Faith and reason in an age of uncertainty', *The Tablet* (6 July 1996), p. 893.

Chapter 9

1. Dorothee Soelle, *Theology for Sceptics* (Mowbray, London, 1995), p. 107.

2.   Robert J. Schreiter, *Constructing Local Theologies* (SCM Pr ss, London, 1985), p. 29.

3.   This chapter is adapted in part from an article of mine entitled 'Inculturation: some theological perspectives', published in *International Review of Mission* (Vol. 85, 1996), 173–80.

4.   *Collectanea S. C. Progaganda Fide*, I, p. 42, n. 135.

5.   Joseph Ratzinger, 'Christ, Faith and the Challenge of Cultures' [Hong Kong Speech of March 1993], *L'Osservatore Romano* (English edition), 26 April 1995, pp. 5–8. Quotations from p. 6.

6.   Cecil McGarry in *What happened at the African Synod*, ed. C. McGarry (Paulines Publications, Nairobi, 1995), p. 188.

7.   Christopher Dawson, *Religion and the Rise of Western Culture* (Sheed & Ward, London, 1950), p. 33.

8.   John Paul II, *Catechesi tradendae*, 1979, No. 53.

9.   *Santo Domingo and Beyond: documents and commentaries from the Fourth General Conference of Latin American Bishops*, ed. Alfred Hennelly, (Orbis Books, Maryknoll, NY, 1993), Nos. 253–4, pp. 142–3.

10. Pope John Paul II, Letter founding the Pontifical Council for Culture, 20 May 1982.

11. *L'Osservatore Romano*, 27 April 1979.

12. The English text of *Ecclesia in Africa* was published in *L'Osservatore Romano*, English weekly edition, 20 September 1995, as well as in a separate booklet from the Vatican Press. Reference to paragraphs of this document will be given in parenthesis in the text.

13. The encyclical *Redemptoris Missio*, No. 54.

14. *Jesuit Apostolates Today*, ed. Jerome Aixala (Institute Jesuit Sources, St Louis, 1981), p. 173.

15. Karl Rahner, *Belief Today* (Sheed & Ward, London, 1973), pp. 48–51.

16. Peter C. Phan, 'Cultural Diversity: a blessing or a curse for theology and spirituality?', *Louvain Studies*, 19 (1994), 195–211. References to pp. 201–202.

17. Aylward Shorter, *Toward a theology of inculturation* (Geoffrey Chapman, London, 1988), pp. 11–12.

18. Speech to Catechetics Congress, 26 September 1992.

19. 'Our Mission and Culture', No. 22, *Documents of the 34th General Congregation of the Society of Jesus* (Institute of Jesuit Sources, St Louis, 1995), p. 60.

Chapter 10

1.   Margaret Archer, *Culture and Agency*, op. cit., p. xxii.

2.   Tony Kelly, *Consuming Passions: Christianity and the Consumer Society* (Australian Catholic Bishops Conference, Sydney, 1995), p. 11.

3. Michael Paul Gallagher, *Help my Unbelief*, revised edition (Veritas, Dublin, 1987), p. 46.

4. Josep Vives, 'Dios en el crepusculo del siglo XX', *Razón y Fe* (Vol. 223, 1991), pp. 467–79. Quotation from p. 468. [The play on words exists also in Spanish: 'Falta Dios pero no se le echa en falta'.]

5. James McAuley, 'A Letter to John Dryden', in *Anthology of Australian Religious Poetry*, ed. Les Murray (Collins Dove, North Blackburn, 1991), p. 168.

6. This echoes the insights of Stephen Carter, already cited in the Introduction.

7. William Barry, 'U.S. Culture and Contemporary Spirituality', *Review for Religions* (Vol. 54, 1995), p. 7.

8. Rafael Esteban, 'Evangelization, Culture and Spirituality', *The Way* (Vol. 34, 1994), pp. 274–5.

9. J. H. Newman, *Grammar of Assent* (Longman, London, 1901), pp. 92–3.

10. T. S. Eliot, *On Poetry and Poets* (Faber & Faber, London, 1957), p. 25.

11. Andrew Greeley, *Religion: a secular theory* (New York, 1982), p. 48. See also his more recent book *Religion and Poetry* (Transaction Publishers, New York, 1995).

12. John Milbank, *Theology and Social Theory: Beyond Secular Reason* (Basil Blackwell, Oxford, 1990), pp. 380–81, 422.

13. H. Richard Niebuhr, *Christ and Culture* (Harper, New York, 1956).

14. Speech of 11 October 1962, in *The Documents of Vatican II*, ed. Walter Abbott (Geoffrey Chapman, London, 1966), p. 712.

15. Seamus Murphy, '*Evangelii nuntiandi* Twenty Years After: Culture, Pluralism and Secularism', *Milltown Studies* (No. 37, Spring 1996), pp. 82–107. Quotation from p. 84.

16. See Ph. Bossuyt and J. Rademakers, 'Rencontre de l'Incroyant et Inculturation: Paul à Athènes (Ac. 17, 16–34)', *Nouvelle Revue Théologique* (CXVII, 1995), pp. 19–43.

17. Charles Taylor, *The Ethics of Authenticity* (Harvard University Press, Cambridge, 1991), p. 94.

18. 'Our Mission and Culture' (No. 9), *Documents of the 34th General Congregation of the Society of Jesus* (Institute of Jesuit Sources, St Louis, 1995), p. 54.

Chapter 11

1. Sebastian Moore, *God is a New Language* (Darton, Longman and Todd, London, 1967), p. 56.

2. Riccardo Tonelli, unpublished paper on Youth Ministry, given at a European Symposium in Rome, May 1994 (my translation).

3. Quoted by Michael Warren, *Faith, Culture and the Worshipping Community*, revised edition (Pastoral Press, Washington, DC, 1993), p. 160.

4. Michael Warren, *Youth, Gospel, Liberation*, 2nd edition (Don Bosco Multimedia, New Rochelle, 1994), p. 143.

5. John F. Kavanaugh, *Following Christ in a Consumer Society: The Spirituality of Cultural Resistance*, revised edition (Orbis Books, New York, 1991), p. 21.

6. *ibid.*, p. 113.

7. Michael Warren, *Communications and Cultural Analysis* (Bergin & Garvey, Westport, Conn., 1992), p. 118.

8. Kavanaugh, *op. cit.*, p. 165.

9. Michael Warren, 'The Material Conditions of Our Seeing and Perceiving', *New Theology Review* (Vol. 7, 1994), pp. 37–59. Quotation from p. 57.

10. *Communications and Cultural Analysis*, pp. 6, 16.

11. Michael Warren, 'Youth Evangelization and Counter-Evangelization', *Living Light* (Fall 1993), pp. 42–51. Quotation from p. 43.

12. *Faith, Culture and the Worshipping Community*, p. xii.

13. Kavanaugh, *op. cit.*, p. 162.

14. *Youth, Gospel, Liberation*, p. 152.

15. Kieran Flanagan, *The Enchantment of Sociology: A Study of Theology and Culture* (Macmillan, London, 1996), p. 226.

16. *ibid.*, p. 54.

17. *ibid.*, p. 158.

18. *Communications and Cultural Analysis*, pp. 8–9.

19. Kavanaugh, *op. cit.*, p. 127.

20. *Communications and Cultural Analysis*, p. 13.

21. *Gospel, Youth, Liberation*, p. 153.

22. Ludwig Wittgenstein, *Culture and Value*, ed. G. H. von Wright (Blackwell, Oxford, 1980), p. 64.

23. Kavanaugh, *op. cit.*, p. 137.

Chapter 12

1. Veronica Brady, 'Postmodernism and the Spiritual Life', *The Way* (Vol. 36, 1996), p. 179.

2. C. John Somerville, *The Secularization of Early Modern England: from religious culture to religious faith* (Oxford University Press, New York, 1992), p. 9.

3. Seamus Heaney, *Station Island* (Faber & Faber, London, 1984), p. 118. It seems appropriate to begin this final chapter with a text from 'creative culture'. This artistic dimension has been somewhat neglected in this book because of the vastly increased attention given to 'lived culture' in recent years in religious and theological circles. On another occasion I hope to write about the dialogue of faith with the world of literary imagination.

4. This expression was first used by John Paul II in Port-au-Prince, 3 March 1983.

5. See Donal Dorr, *Divine Energy* (Gill & Macmillan, Dublin, 1996).

6. The quoted phrases here come from Charles Taylor, 'Spirituality of Life – and Its Shadow', *Compass* (Toronto, May–June 1996), p. 12.

7. Sandra Schneiders, 'Spirituality in the Academy', *Theological Studies* (Vol. 50, 1989), p. 684.

8. Philip Sheldrake, *Spirituality and History* (SPCK, London, 1991), pp. 37, 52.

9. James J. Bacik, *Spirituality in Transition* (Sheed & Ward, Kansas, 1996), pp. 5–6.

10. Michael Kearney, *Mortally Wounded: Stories of Soul Pain, Death and Healing* (Marino Books, Dublin, 1996), pp. 60, 63. These insights from a consultant in palliative medicine, writing mainly about therapy with the terminally ill, are also applicable to a larger spiritual crisis in our culture. I had the pleasure of discussing this point with Dr Kearney, who was in agreement with this broadening of the agenda from the personal to the cultural.

11. See my article 'Apologetics: towards a different agenda', *Priests and People* (Vol. 9, 1995), 367–71.

12. Vaclav Havel, 'Postmodern world needs new principle' [Philadelphia Speech], *Arizona Daily Star*, 8 July 1994.

13. William D. Dinges, 'Postmodernism and Religious Institutions', *The Way* (Vol. 36, 1996), pp. 218–219.

14. James Bacik, *op. cit.*, pp. 22, 31, 43–5, 49.

15. Ronald Rolheiser, *The Shattered Lantern*, (Hodder & Stoughton, London, 1994), p. 45.

16. Paul Tillich, *Systematic Theology*, Volume III (University of Chicago Press, Chicago, 1963), pp. 158, 246.

17. Flanagan, *The Enchantment of Sociology*, p. 17.

18. Hans Urs von Balthasar with Angelo Scola, *Test Everything: Hold Fast to What is Good* (Ignatius Press, San Francisco, 1989), p. 25.

19. *ibid.*, pp. 26, 50, 52.

Epilogue

1. Letter of 1843, quoted in Ian Ker, *John Henry Newman: a biography* (Oxford University Press, Oxford, 1988), p. 273.

2. Robert Wuthnow, *Christianity in the Twenty-first Century* (Oxford University Press, Oxford, 1993), p. 14.

3. See the eloquent argument on community and family by Jonathan Sacks in his book *Faith in the Future* (Darton, Longman & Todd, 1994).

4. See Robert M. Doran, *Theology and the Dialectics of History* (University of Toronto Press, Toronto, 1990), p. 134.

5. Bernard Lonergan, *A Third Collection*, ed. F. E. Crowe (Geoffrey Chapman, London, 1985), p. 158.

Select Bibliography

Arbuckle, Gerald A., *Earthing the Gospel: an inculturation handbook for pastoral workers* (Geoffrey Chapman, London, 1990).

——, *Refounding the Church* (Geoffrey Chapman, London, 1993).

Archer, Margaret, *Culture and Agency: the place of culture in social theory* (Cambridge University Press, Cambridge, 1988).

Ariarajah, S. Wesley, *Gospel and Culture: An Ongoing Discussion within the Ecumenical Movement* (Gospel and Cultures Pamphlet 1, WCC Publications, Geneva, 1994).

Bacik, James J., *Spirituality in Transition* (Sheed & Ward, Kansas, 1996).

Barry, William, 'U.S. Culture and Contemporary Spirituality', *Review for Religious* (Vol. 54, 1995), 6–21.

Bourdieu, Pierre, et al., *Academic Discourse* (Polity Press, Cambridge, 1994).

Brady, Veronica, 'Postmodernism and the Spiritual Life', *The Way* (Vol. 36, 1996), 179–87.

Carrier, Hervé, *Evangelizing the Culture of Modernity* (Orbis Books, New York, 1993).

Carter, Stephen L., *The Culture of Disbelief: how American Law and Politics Trivialize Religious Devotion* (Basic Books, New York, 1993).

Casanova, José, *Public Religions in the Modern World* (University of Chicago Press, Chicago, 1994).

Cassidy, Eoin G., ed., *Faith and Culture in the Irish Context* (Veritas Publications, Dublin, 1996).

Dawson, Christopher, *Religion and Culture* (Sheed & Ward, London, 1948).

Douglas, Mary, *Natural Symbols: Explorations in Cosmology* (Cresset Press, London, 1970).

——, *Risk and Blame: essays in cultural theory* (Routledge, London, 1992).

——, *In the Wilderness* (Academic Press, Sheffield, 1993).

Doran, Robert, *Theology and the Dialectics of History* (University of Toronto Press, Toronto, 1990).

Dupré, Louis, *Passage to Modernity* (Yale University Press, New Haven, 1993).

Eliot, T. S., *Notes towards the Definition of Culture* (Faber & Faber, London, 1948).

Esteban, Rafael, 'Evangelization, Culture and Spirituality', *The Way* (Vol. 34, 1994), 273–82.

Flanagan, Kieran, *The Enchantment of Sociology: A Study of Theology and Culture* (Macmillan, London, 1996).

Gallagher, Michael Paul, *What are they saying about unbelief?* (Paulist, New York, 1995).

——, *Free to Believe*, revised edition (Darton, Longman & Todd, London, 1996).

Geertz, Clifford, *The Interpretation of Cultures* (Basic Books, New York, 1973).

——, *Local Knowledge: Further Essays in Interpretive Anthropology* (Basic Books, New York, 1983).

Gibbons, Luke, *Transformations in Irish Culture* (Cork University Press, Cork, 1996).

Giddens, Anthony, *The Consequences of Modernity* (Polity Press, Cambridge, 1990).

Graham, Elaine L., *Transforming Practice: Pastoral Theology in an Age of Uncertainty* (Mowbray, London, 1996).

Greeley, Andrew, *Religion and Poetry* (Transaction Publishers, New York, 1995).

Gremillion, Joseph, ed., *The Church and Culture since Vatican II*, (University of Notre Dame Press, Notre Dame, 1985).

Guardini, Romano, *The End of the Modern World* (Sheed & Ward, London, 1951).

——, *Letters from Lake Como* (Ressourcement edition, William Eerdmans, Grand Rapids, 1994).

Hennelly, Alfred, ed., *Santo Domingo and Beyond* (Orbis Books, New York, 1993).

Huntington, Samuel, 'The Clash of Civilizations?', *Foreign Affairs*, (Summer 1993), 22–49.

Inglis, Fred, *Cultural Studies* (Blackwell, Oxford, 1993).

Johnson, Elizabeth, 'Between the Times: religious life and the postmodern experience of God', *Review for Religious* (Vol. 53, 1994), 6–28.

Kavanaugh, John F., *Following Christ in a Consumer Society: The Spirituality of Cultural Resistance*, revised edition (Orbis Books, New York, 1991).

Kearney, Michael, *Mortally Wounded: Stories of Soul Pain, Death and Healing* (Marino Books, Dublin, 1996).

Kolakowski, Leszek, *Modernity on Endless Trial* (University of Chicago Press, Chicago, 1990).

Kroeber, A. L. and Kluckhohn, Clyde, *Culture: A Critical Review of Concepts and Definitions* (Vintage Books, New York, 1963).

Lane, Dermot, ed., *Religion and Culture in Dialogue* (Columba Press, Dublin, 1993).

Llano, Alejandro, *La nuova sensibilità: il positivo della società postmoderna* (Ares, Milan, 1995).

Lonergan, Bernard, *Insight: a study of human understanding* (Longman Green, London, 1958).

——, *Method in Theology* (Darton, Longman & Todd, London, 1972).

Luzbetak, Louis J., *The Church and Cultures* (Divine Word Publications, Techny, 1970).

Miguens, Fernando, *Fe y Cultura en la Enseñanza de Juan Pablo II* (Ediciones Palabra, Madrid, 1994).

Milbank, John, *Theology and Social Theory: Beyond Secular Reason* (Basil Blackwell, Oxford, 1990).

Montefiore, Hugh, ed., *The Gospel and Contemporary Culture* (Mowbray, London, 1992).

Murphy, Seamus, '*Evangelii nuntiandi* Twenty Years After: Culture, Pluralism and Secularism', *Milltown Studies* (No. 37, Spring 1996), 82–107.

Newbigin, Lesslie, *Foolishness to the Greeks* (SPCK, London, 1986).

——, *Gospel in a Pluralist Society* (SPCK, London, 1989).

Niebuhr, H. Richard, *Christ and Culture* (Harper, New York, 1956).

Ong, Walter J., *Orality and Literacy: the Technologizing of the Word* (Routledge, London, 1982).

——, *Faith and Contexts* [Collected Essays 1952–91], 2 vols, ed. Thomas Farrell (Scholars Press, Atlanta, 1992).

Osborn, Lawrence, *Restoring the Vision: the Gospel and Modern Culture* (Mowbray, London, 1995).

Osmond, Rosalie, *Changing Perspectives: Christian Culture and Morals in England Today* (Darton, Longman & Todd, London, 1993).

Poupard, Paul, *The Church and Culture: Challenge and Confrontation* (Central Bureau CCVA, St Louis, 1994).

Raiser, Konrad, 'Gospel and Cultures', *International Review of Mission* (Vol. 83, No. 331, 1994), 623–9.

Rolheiser, Ronald, *The Shattered Lantern*, (Hodder & Stoughton, London, 1994).

Roest Crollius, Ary, *What is so new about Inculturation?* (Gregorian University Press, Rome, 1984).

Sacks, Jonathan, *Faith in the Future* (Darton, Longman & Todd, London, 1995).

Schindler, David L., ed., *Catholicism and Secularization in America: Essays on Nature, Grace, and Culture* (Communio Books, Notre Dame, 1990).

Schneiders, Sandra, 'Spirituality in the Academy', *Theological Studies* (Vol. 50, 1989), 676–97.

Schreiter, Robert J., *Constructing Local Theologies* (SCM Press, London 1985).

Shorter, Aylward, *Towards a theology of inculturation* (Geoffrey Chapman, London, 1988).

Somerville, C. John, *The Secularization of Early Modern England: from religious culture to religious faith* (Oxford University Press, New York, 1992).

Taylor, Charles, *Sources of the Self: the making of modern identity* (Harvard University Press, Cambridge, 1989).

——, *The Ethics of Authenticity* (Harvard University Press, Cambridge, 1991).

Tillich, Paul, *A Theology of Culture* (Oxford University Press, New York, 1959).

Touraine, Alain, *Critique of Modernity* (Blackwell, Oxford, 1995).

Tracy, David, 'Theology and the Many Faces of Postmodernity', *Theology Today*, (Vol. 51, 1994), 104–114.

Walsh, David, *After Ideology: Recovering the Spiritual Foundations of Freedom* (Catholic University of America Press, Washington, DC, 1990).

Warren, Michael, *Faith, Culture and the Worshipping Community* (Pastoral Press, Washington, DC, 1993).

——, *Communications and Cultural Analysis* (Bergin & Garvey, Westport, Conn., 1992).

——, *Youth, Gospel, Liberation*, 2nd edition (Don Bosco Multimedia, New Rochelle, 1994).

Williams, Raymond, *Culture* (Fontana, London, 1981).

——, *Culture and Society* (Hogarth Press, London, 1993).

——, *The Long Revolution* (Chatto & Windus, London, 1961).

Wuthnow, Robert, *Christianity in the Twenty-first Century* (Oxford University Press, Oxford, 1993).

Yuhaus, Cassian, ed., *The Catholic Church and American Culture* (Paulist Press, New York, 1990).